# PRAISE FOR DEBUNKING 9/11 MYTHS

"*Debunking 9/11 Myths* is a reliable and rational answer to the many fanciful conspiracy theories about 9/11. Despite the fact that the myths are fictitious, many have caught on with those who do not trust their government to tell the truth anymore. Fortunately, the government is not sufficiently competent to pull off such conspiracies and too leaky to keep them secret. What happened on 9/11 has been well established by the 9/11 Commission. What did *not* happen has now been clearly explained by *Popular Mechanics*."

—RICHARD A. CLARKE, former national security advisor, author of *Against All Enemies: Inside America's War on Terror*

"This book is a victory for common sense; 9/11 conspiracy theorists beware: *Popular Mechanics* has popped your paranoid bubble world, using pointed facts and razor-sharp analysis.

—AUSTIN BAY, national security columnist (Creators Syndicate), author (with James F. Dunnigan) of *From Shield to Storm: High-Tech Weapons, Military Strategy and Coalition Warfare in the Persian Gulf*

"Even though I study weird beliefs for a living, I never imagined that the 9/11 conspiracy theories that cropped up shortly after that tragic event would ever get cultural traction in America, but here we are with a plethora of conspiracies and no end in sight. What we need is a solid work of straightforward debunking, and now we have it in *Debunking 9/11 Myths*. The *Popular Mechanics* article upon which the book is based was one of the finest works of investigative journalism and skeptical analysis that I have ever encountered, and the book-length treatment of this codswallop will stop the conspiracy theorists in their fantasy-prone tracks. A brilliant exemplar of critical thinking."

—MICHAEL SHERMER, publisher, *Skeptic* magazine; monthly columnist for *Scientific American*; author of *Why People Believe Weird Things*

"A small but vocal and opinionated segment of the population of questionable technical qualifications and obscure personal motivations is obsessed with, and actively disseminates, harebrained explanations for the "true causes" of the terrorist attack of 9/11. *Popular Mechanics* does an invaluable and laudable service by providing a meticulous analysis and documentation of the unfortunate events that took place five years ago. This book demonstrates convincingly the complete lack of substance of the allegations on the involvement of the U.S. government in this affair. A must-read for all those still in doubt!"
—EDUARDO KAUSEL, professor of civil and environmental engineering, Massachusetts Institute of Technology

"Based on exhaustive research, *Debunking 9/11 Myths* is a testament to American competence and honesty. The description of the mythmakers who spin fantasies on the Internet makes for compelling reading."
—BING WEST, former assistant secretary of defense, author of *No True Glory: A Frontline Account of the Battle for Fallujah*

"All too often the scientific community is prone to ignore the nonsensical claims of the conspiracy theorists as not being worthy of a reply. However, something important is lost in taking such an idealistic position. The public, who may not be acquainted with many of the more detailed facts surrounding the events of 9/11, may not be in a position to immediately see the fallacy in what is put forward by conspiracy theorists as evidence, on Web sites and on the radio. By addressing the more popular conspiracy theories, and pointing out their many serious flaws and shortcomings, *Debunking 9/11 Myths* serves the public through this defense of common sense."
—CHRISTOPHER J. EARLS, associate professor of civil and environmental engineering, Cornell University

"David Dunbar and Brad Reagan shine the cold light of reason on conspiracy theories that have been festering since the awful day of September 11. It's a necessary antidote to toxic propaganda."
—GLENN REYNOLDS, professor of law, University of Tennessee, Instapundit.com blogger, and author of *An Army of Davids: How Markets and Technology Empower Ordinary People to Beat Big Media, Big Government, and Other Goliaths*

# DEBUNKING 9/11 MYTHS

## WHY CONSPIRACY THEORIES CAN'T STAND UP TO THE FACTS

**INCLUDES NEW FINDINGS ON WORLD TRADE CENTER BUILDING 7**

FOREWORD BY
**JAMES B. MEIGS**

EDITED BY
**DAVID DUNBAR & BRAD REAGAN**

AN IN-DEPTH INVESTIGATION BY
**PopularMechanics**

HEARST BOOKS
New York

**HEARST BOOKS**
New York

An Imprint of Sterling Publishing
387 Park Avenue South
New York, NY 10016

This book was previously published in 2006 under the title *Debunking 9/11 Myths*. Information from the 2006 edition, including names, titles, and locations has been updated where central to new content, but left otherwise untouched.

Editor-in-Chief, Popular Mechanics: James B. Meigs
Editors: David Dunbar and Brad Reagan
Contributing Editor for the Revised Edition: Davin Coburn
Reporters/Writers: Arianne Cohen and Christian DeBenedetti
Cover design: Peter Herbert and Agustin Chung
Interior Design: Celia Fuller
Photography Editors: Allyson Torrisi and Sarah Shatz
Project Editor: Catharine Wells and Alyssa Smith
Researchers: Davin Coburn and Tyghe Trimble

Library of Congress Cataloging-in-Publication Data available upon request.

10  9  8  7  6  5  4  3  2  1

Popular Mechanics is a registered trademark of Hearst Communications, Inc.

www.popularmechanics.com

For information about custom editions, special sales, premium and corporate purchases, please contact Sterling Special Sales Department at 800-805-5489 or specialsales@sterlingpublishing.com.

Distributed in Canada by Sterling Publishing
c/o Canadian Manda Group, 165 Dufferin Street
Toronto, Ontario, Canada M6K 3H6

Distributed in Australia by Capricorn Link (Australia) Pty. Ltd.
P.O. Box 704, Windsor, NSW 2756 Australia

Printed in USA

Sterling ISBN 978-1-58816-547-3

# CONTENTS

# ACKNOWLEDGMENTS
## TO THE ORIGINAL EDITION

In late 2004, when *Popular Mechanics* decided to examine 9/11 conspiracy theories, the magazine's editors brought in a team of writers and reporters to tackle what became an intense, complex project. Their work, published in the March 2005 issue as "9/11: Debunking the Myths," provided the foundation for this book. Thanks go to the members of the original reporting team—Benjamin Chertoff, Davin Coburn, Michael Connery, David Enders, Kevin Haynes, Kristin Roth, Tracy Saelinger, and Erik Sofge—as well as the talented editors, designers, and photography editors on staff who helped pull it all together.

When *Popular Mechanics* decided to expand the cover story into a book, Arianne Cohen and Christian DeBenedetti came on board to enhance and update the magazine reporting and tackle new theories. Without their skillful writing and pinpoint reporting, this book would not have been possible.

Under the guidance and supervision of director of photography Allyson Torrisi, researcher Sarah Shatz dug through thousands of photographs taken on 9/11 and the days afterward to find the right images to complement the reporting for the magazine story. Allyson and Sarah did such a tremendous job that we asked them to team up again to find more material for the book. We are also grateful to other *Popular Mechanics* staffers who, like Allyson, willingly added to their magazine workload to help us complete the project: design director Michael Lawton, who oversaw the compelling cover design of senior art director Peter Herbert and designer Agustin Chung; research editor Davin Coburn, who scrutinized the text for accuracy (any errors remain our responsibility); researcher Tyghe Trimble for pulling together the appendixes, and assistant to the editor-in-chief Erin McCarthy, who coordinated advance reviews.

We also owe a large debt of gratitude to Hearst Books: vice president and publisher Jacqueline Deval for her early and unflagging support, associate project editor Catharine Wells for her editorial and organizational skills, design director Celia Fuller for her elegant layouts, and copy editor Christine Furry for her discerning reading of the manuscript.

Above all, we'd like to thank the hundreds of engineers, investigators, scientists, officials, eyewitnesses, and survivors who gave their time to help us clarify the facts. As many of them have learned, taking a public stance in defense of the facts of 9/11 can make one a target of accusations, invective, and even threats from supporters of "alternative" theories. Our sources' commitment to helping answer the questions of 9/11 is commendable.                               —The Editors

# FOREWORD

## By James B. Meigs,
### Editor-in-Chief of *Popular Mechanics*

*Popular Mechanics* set out to investigate conspiracy theories about the 9/11 attacks in late 2004, just as those claims were emerging from the swamps of extremist websites and radical Islamist organizations. We had no idea how much trouble we were about to stir up. Our first magazine article on the topic, which appeared in the March 2005 issue, closely examined the major scientific, military, aeronautical, and engineering-based claims commonly cited as evidence that 9/11 was, as conspiracy theorists like to say, an inside job. Our investigation found no evidence in support of the conspiracy claims—but many cases in which facts cited by the theorists had been deliberately twisted.

The article unleashed a flood of criticisms and accusations from those supporting such theories. These attacks ranged from the preposterous (it was said our magazine had published this investigation on orders from a cabal of Masons and Illuminati) to alarming (death threats were referred to our security department). Clearly, we had touched a nerve. The article quickly became the most widely read story in the history of *Popular Mechanics'* Web site, with over 7.5 million views. (A detailed account of the reaction to our article, and what that reaction says about the conspiracy movement, can be found in the original afterword to this book on page 121.)

A team of *Popular Mechanics* reporters and editors then started work on a far more detailed book-length version of the report. By the time the first edition of this book was published in the summer of 2006, the 9/11 conspiracy furor was reaching a tipping point. The flurry of books on the topic had grown into an avalanche, with certain writers, such as former Claremont School of Theology professor David Ray Griffin, building a thriving cottage industry around the topic. Conspiracy fans had, with Orwellian overtones, taken to calling themselves "the 9/11 Truth Movement," or simply "truthers." Extremist talk radio programs such as *The Alex Jones Show* pushed the issue nonstop. And a video pastiche of conspiracy theories, a quasi-documentary known as *Loose Change*, was becoming an Internet sensation. The film's director, an aspiring filmmaker from Oneonta, NY, named Dylan Avery, would eventually produce several versions of the film with various collaborators. Avery and his colleagues showed little aptitude for fact-checking, but real talent as propagandists. The various editions of *Loose Change* would go on to become some of the most widely viewed films in the history of the Internet.

At that time, as today, it was my view that the facts surrounding September 11, 2001, matter. It was a momentous day, one in which nearly 3,000 civilians died, and one that would shape U.S. and world history. The political response to 9/11 brought about significant changes in U.S. law and in the structure of our federal agencies. The two wars it spawned drag on to this day. It is hard to imagine a recent historical event more important for Americans to understand accurately. If there was even the slightest truth to the allegations raised by 9/11 conspiracy theorists, those facts would be of the gravest geopolitical and historical importance.

*Popular Mechanics'* 9/11 project represented one of the relatively few attempts by mainstream journalists to grapple seriously with the conspiracy theory claims. So it was telling that most conspiracy theorists—who are eager to repeat any shred of mainstream reporting they believe bolsters their claims—quickly decided that *Popular Mechanics* too was part of the conspiracy. In their minds, all our research could therefore be rejected a *priori*. We had run head on into a worldview that some experts call "conspiracism." It is a mindset that insists on reaching a predetermined conclusion regardless of what information is presented. Any facts that don't fit the conspiracy paradigm need to be explained away. Since 2004, leading 9/11 theorist David Ray Griffin has written seven books and edited two others on the subject of 9/11. He devoted a chapter in his book, *Debunking 9/11 Debunking: An Answer to* Popular Mechanics *and Other Defenders of the Official Conspiracy Theory*, to explain why, in his view, the 9/11 reporting by *Popular Mechanics* and other mainstream journalists is invalid.

Griffin's book devotes many pages to the idea that *Popular Mechanics* and our parent company, the Hearst Corporation, are somehow implicated in the vast conspiracy he sees behind

9/11. He digs up century-old controversies and finds tenuous links between the magazine's staff and various government officials. But he never explains how a magazine—much less a major corporation—could possibly convince its employees to help cover up the most notorious mass murder in our nation's history. *Popular Mechanics* has close to 30 editorial staffers and dozens of freelance contributors. Does Griffin imagine that whenever we hire new editors I bring them into a secret bunker and initiate them into an ultraclandestine society for world domination? Why wouldn't such prospective employees run screaming from our building? In the years since we began our work on 9/11 conspiracy theories, a number of our staffers have moved on to other jobs. What would stop them from revealing a conspiracy that, if true, would be one of the biggest journalistic scoops in history? Did we swear them all to secrecy? As with so many conspiracy claims, the whole elaborate fantasy becomes practically laughable on close examination.

On the one hand, it's understandable that many journalists saw these overheated theories as being too marginal to take seriously. But on the other, it is unfortunate that so few media outlets bothered to address the many clearly erroneous claims of the conspiracy set. Their reluctance to enter the fray gave conspiracy theorists access to uncontested ground. As this book documents, many conspiracy claims rely on snippets of material from mainstream media outlets. As a rule, these snippets have been quoted wildly out of context or reflect minor errors in initial reports that were later superseded by more accurate reporting. But, when the news organizations that published or broadcast these accounts failed to challenge flatly deceptive interpretations of their work, it allowed conspiracy theorists to add a veneer of credibility to their fanciful claims.

As a result, a vague sense that there might be some truth to conspiracy theorists' claims began to seep into American popular culture. Individually, many examples of how the conspiracist mind-set infiltrates our culture are fairly minor, even silly. But they add up. In 2007, Rosie O'Donnell, then one of the hosts of ABC's *The View*, endorsed the theory that pre-planted explosives were involved in the collapse of World Trade Center 7. (Attacking the mainstream account that heat from fires weakened the structure, O'Donnell showed her passion for the topic—and her limited knowledge of basic metallurgy—in saying, "I do believe that it's the first time in history that fire has ever melted steel.") In 2009, the FX show *Rescue Me*, starring Denis Leary and about a fictional group of New York City firefighters, aired an episode that focused on conspiracy talking points. The storyline centers on a character played by actor Daniel Sunjata, who strongly believes that "9/11 was an inside job."

Other celebrities whose supportive statements have lit up conspiracy blogs in recent years include Janeane Garofalo, Roseanne Barr, Woody Harrelson, Willie Nelson, Charlie Sheen, and 2011 Academy Award nominee Mark Ruffalo, who recently told conspiracy-minded group "We Are Change," "I don't want to jump to any conclusions, but I also don't think that it's ever been given its due diligence considering that it's the largest crime ever committed on U.S. soil." And in February, seven-time Emmy Award winner Ed Asner put out a YouTube casting call for a new movie titled "Confessions of a 9/11 Conspirator." The script, he says, is based on Griffin's research and proves that, "The official accounts issued . . . have been proven without any doubt whatsoever to be one big lie from start to finish." Actors like Harrelson and Sheen might not be poster boys for clear-headed thinking—but that doesn't mean their words aren't embraced and amplified by the conspiracy set.

Conspiracy theories also began to creep into our national politics. Cynthia McKinney, who served six terms in the U.S. House of Representatives as a Democrat, and who was nominated as the Green Party candidate for president in 2008, was an early and outspoken adherent to the conspiracist view of 9/11. In 2005, she invited Griffin to address the Congressional Black Caucus on the topic. Advocates of conspiracy theories were a prominent, if little noted, component of antiwar and other left-leaning gatherings through most of the past decade. ("I'm a 9/11 truther," antiwar icon Cindy Sheehan recently announced.) But fondness for conspiracy theories is not a strictly partisan affair. During his 2008 presidential run, Libertarian Ron Paul also seemed to include a disproportionate share of conspiracy fans among his eclectic group of supporters. And in January, former Libertarian Party of Nevada chair Jim Duensing announced that he would seek his party's nomination for the presidency in 2012. Duensing—who that same month held a Martin Luther King, Jr. Day rally at a shooting range—is the founder of Libertarians for Justice, which demands "justice" for "researchers and experts who have dedicated their lives to researching the government's conspiracy theory" about 9/11.

The issue reached the White House in 2009, when it was revealed that Van Jones, the Obama administration's special advisor for green jobs, had apparently signed a petition circulated by www.911truth.org charging that the Bush administration "may indeed have deliberately allowed 9/11 to happen." After much controversy, Jones resigned in September of that year from the White House Council on Environmental Quality.

Conspiracy theories generally get a much more sympathetic reception overseas. Griffin and other leading theorists frequently tour Europe and Asia, where arguments that the United States engineered the deaths of its own citizens often meet with a positive response. International polls have shown that, in many countries, the evidence showing that Al Qaeda carried out the attacks fails to persuade the majority of citizens. For example, according to one poll, only 39 percent of the population of U.S. ally Turkey blames Al Qaeda for the attacks, while 36 percent believes the U.S. was responsible. In Egypt, 16 percent of the public attributes the attacks to Al Qaeda, but 43 percent believes Israel was behind the events. Iranian president Mahmoud Ahmadinejad alludes to 9/11 conspiracy theories in speeches, including ones delivered at the United Nations and in other international settings.

Given that Al Qaeda, and bin Laden himself, repeatedly took credit for the attacks, the wide support for conspiracy theories overseas is troubling. The death of bin Laden at the hands of U. S. forces in May 2011 seems unlikely to change that dynamic. Regardless of one's view of U.S. foreign policy, the fact that such theories leave our allies confused—and enemies emboldened—cannot be good for America's long-term interests.

In the U.S., the rising tide of 9/11 conspiracism has seemed to slow, and perhaps even abate, in recent years.

*Popular Mechanics'* work on the issue has been a key part of that process. Since our original article was published, some of the more far-fetched conspiracy claims have increasingly fallen out of favor with theorists themselves: for example, the notion that a missile, not an airplane, struck the Pentagon; and the idea that the aircraft that struck World Trade Center 2 had a military "pod" bulging from the fuselage. Of course, dedicated conspiracists rarely rethink their conclusions, no matter how often the facts supporting those conclusions turn out to be false. The original *Popular Mechanics* article addressed 16 of the most common 9/11 conspiracy claims. The first edition of this book expanded that list by four, and added much more detail. As a result, many of the more adept theorists simply moved on to new theories, or shifted their focus to issues that our team had not covered as deeply. For example, at the time we published the first edition, there was still no definitive account of why World Trade Center 7— which was not hit by planes, only damaged by debris—also collapsed. Not surprisingly, as the truther community moved away from talk about missiles and pods, it began focusing obsessively on elaborate theories concerning WTC 7. (With the benefit of much more detailed engineering analysis, this edition addresses—and debunks—those WTC 7 claims in depth.)

It is hard to argue without facts. And yet that is the position in which 9/11 conspiracists increasingly find themselves. One by one, the key factual underpinnings of their theories have been demolished. But still they argue on, their passionate conviction undiminished, until they've come to resemble the Black Knight in the famous scene from the film *Monty*

*Python and the Holy Grail.* Overmatched in a swordfight, the knight loses one arm, then the other, then both legs to stand on. But he is undeterred, shouting, "It's just a flesh wound!"

In the end, the truther community's tendency toward unintentional self-parody has perhaps done as much to undermine its credibility as has the work of *Popular Mechanics.* Just when the conspiracy movement seemed to be making real headway toward deeply influencing American culture, a funny thing happened: it began to turn into a punch line. *South Park* offered a brutal parody of the conspiracist worldview in an episode called "Mystery of the Urinal Deuce." Comedian Jon Stewart started tweaking truthers on *The Daily Show,* at one point holding up a sign reading "9/11 WAS AN OUTSIDE JOB." And, in a common-sense answer to the vast legion of conspiracy-oriented websites, an assortment of sharp, and often satirical, blogs has emerged to challenge the truthers on their own turf. In particular, the blog *Screw Loose Change* offers devastating analysis of the truther community, and links to point-by-point rebuttals to the claims advanced in *Loose Change.*

Of course, conspiracy theories involving 9/11 will never fully go away. And a book like this, no matter how widely reported or carefully updated, will never convince the most dedicated conspiracists. But, on the eve of the tenth anniversary of the September 11 attacks, it is important to have a clear, objective, and thorough response to the consistently false and deeply malicious claims of the conspiracy movement. And that's what this book aims to do. As journalists, our highest responsibility is to help the public understand the facts. Over the years that *Popular Mechanics* has been involved in this issue, more than two dozen researchers, reporters, and others at the magazine have helped in this enterprise. In particular, *Popular Mechanics* executive editor David Dunbar has led the project from its earliest days, and contributing editor Davin Coburn has supervised the vast reporting effort required to complete the job. My thanks go out to each of them, as well as to the hundreds of sources who've given us their time and expertise, and in the process, often exposed themselves to attacks from extremists.

Like so many others, I was in New York on September 11, 2001. I'm proud to have played a small part in ensuring that the events of that day are remembered honestly and well.

New York City
2011

# INTRODUCTION

On September 29, 2009, a convoy of 25 tractor-trailers wound through the hills of western Maryland, then turned north. The trucks were decorated with American flags, along with banners that read, "Never Forget 9/11." The National Institute of Standards and Technology (NIST), was returning 250 tons of steel to New York City.

Each piece of mangled metal, collected from the wreckage of the World Trade Center towers, had been meticulously cataloged and studied in Gaithersburg, Maryland, as part of the organization's multiyear investigation into what was not only the most horrific terrorist attack in United States history, but also the nation's worst building disaster. The agency's reports joined a growing chorus of dissertations, engineering analyses, and journal articles describing the probable sequence of events that occurred in Lower Manhattan on the morning of September 11, 2001.

With the release of its *Final Report on the Collapse of World Trade Center Building 7*, NIST's study was complete. The steel hauled north represented a literal and symbolic end to the most massive scientific investigation the agency had ever conducted. But the task of disproving the cacophony of conspiracy theories that surround 9/11 may never end.

The first conspiracy theories began to emerge while the wreckage was still smoldering. As evidence accumulated that conclusively linked the hijackings to Al Qaeda, some self-proclaimed skeptics searched for alternative explanations. Many seemed driven to find a way to blame the United States for somehow abetting, or even orchestrating, the tragedy.

In the years since the attacks, these assertions have grown progressively more lurid and pervasive. If you search the phrase "9/11 conspiracy" on the Internet, you will discover more than one million web pages. A few skeptics make a responsible effort to sift through the mountain of available information, but a vast majority ignore all but a few stray details they think support their theories. In fact, many conspiracy advocates demonstrate a double standard. They distrust the mainstream media coverage and government-sponsored investigations of 9/11, yet they cherry-pick from those same sources to promote their extreme notions: that the hijacked planes weren't commercial jets, but military aircraft, cruise missiles, or remote-control drones; that the World Trade Center buildings were professionally demolished; that American air defenses were deliberately shut down; and more.

*Popular Mechanics* began studying these theories in the fall of 2004, after an advertisement ran in the *New York Times* for the book *Painful Questions* by Eric Hufschmid, demanding that the 9/11 investigation be reopened. Hufschmid's book includes a number of tangible claims regarding 9/11. It states, for example, that because jet fuel does not burn hot enough to melt steel, the fires in the World Trade Center towers could not have caused their collapse. And it claims ample evidence exists to show that demolition-style explosives were pre-positioned in the buildings.

As editors of a magazine devoted to science and technology, we saw these claims as significant. Was there hard evidence to support them? And, if so, what would be the implications for our understanding of 9/11? At the very least, we thought, someone should look into these allegations. If there were even a hint of truth to these or similar claims, then the conspiracy theorists had a point: There should be a deeper investigation.

The magazine assembled a team of reporters and researchers and methodically began to analyze the most common factual claims made by conspiracy theorists—assertions that are at the root of the majority of 9/11 alternative scenarios. We interviewed scores of engineers, aviation experts, military officials, eyewitnesses, and members of the investigative teams—more than 300 sources in all. We pored over photography, maps, blueprints, aviation logs, and transcripts. The results of our research appeared in the March 2005 issue of *Popular Mechanics*. That cover story, "9/11: Debunking the Myths," provoked a strong reaction on the Internet and in the mainstream media.

In the months after we published the investigation, many readers—both critics and supporters—wrote to suggest other evidence they thought we had overlooked or to raise new claims they believed worthy of investigation. Just before the fifth anniversary of 9/11, we reinterviewed experts and sources from our first investigation and produced a book-length version of our findings.

Over the past five years, new theories—and evidence to combat them—have surfaced. With this revision of the book, our team of reporters and researchers debunks the most common speculation about free-fall times, "nano-thermite," and other aspects of the Twin Towers' collapses that began fermenting as the previous book was published. We have dedicated an entire chapter to the many myths surrounding the collapse of World Trade Center Building 7, which initially puzzled even the most qualified investigators. Additionally, we have included new endnotes to point readers to places where they can begin their own informed research, and incorporated new sources. Finally, we have added clarifications to some of our original reporting.

The goal of this book is not to tell the complete story of what happened on September 11, 2001. There are numerous excellent sources, including the 9-11 Commission's report, the National Institute of Standards and Technology reports, and articles in the *New York Times* and other newspapers that chronicle the attacks in painful detail. Instead, this book aims only to answer the questions raised by conspiracy theorists themselves. Strip away the political content and logical leaps, and every conspiracy theory ultimately comes down to a small set of claims based on evidence that can be examined. These claims are the only points where the theorists' elaborate conjectures make contact with the physical world. Without these foundations, the theories crumble. In every case we examined, the key claims made by conspiracy theorists turned out to be mistaken, misinterpreted, or deliberately falsified. We understand that not all conspiracy theorists believe all conspiracy theories. Some prominent theorists even claim that certain theories they deem less plausible have been "planted" in order to make the entire movement look ridiculous. We don't take sides in these debates. We simply check the facts.

The work of comprehending the events of 9/11 is not finished. It is vital to understand the lapses and shortcomings on the part of government agencies in the months and years leading up to 9/11. Every American wishes our government had been more alert and better prepared. And every American is entitled to ask hard questions. But there is a world of difference between believing that our government should have known what was coming and claiming that someone did know and deliberately did nothing—or, even worse, that the government actively perpetrated attacks on its own citizens. By deliberately blurring that line, conspiracy theorists exploit and misdirect the public's legitimate anger and anguish over the events of that day.

Some argue that alternative 9/11 scenarios are valuable in that they promote skepticism of a government that has not always been as open as many would like. But a climate of poisonous suspicion will not help America adjust to the post-9/11 world. And the search for truth is not advanced by the dissemination of falsehoods.

# 1

## THE PLANES

The widely accepted account that hijackers on September 11, 2001, commandeered and crashed four commercial aircraft into the World Trade Center, the Pentagon, and the countryside of southwestern Pennsylvania is supported by reams of evidence, from forensics to passengers' in-flight phone calls to the very basic fact that those on board never returned home. Nonetheless, conspiracy theorists seize on a handful of supposed facts to argue a very different scenario: The jets that struck New York City and Washington D.C. weren't commercial planes, they say, but something else—perhaps refueling tankers or guided missiles. And the lack of military intervention? It clearly proves, they contend, that the U.S. government instigated the assault, or at least allowed it to occur in order to advance oil interests or a war agenda.

One particularly elaborate theory, called "Operation Pearl" (for Pearl Harbor), is found at www.physics911.net. This Web site, which is run by A. K. Dewdney, professor emeritus of computer science at the University of Waterloo in Ontario, reports that U.S. officials ordered the first three passenger jets to land at Harrisburg International Airport, in Pennsylvania, shortly after takeoff. The officials then substituted remote-control aircraft to attack the World Trade Center and the Pentagon.

In order to eliminate witnesses, the passengers were shuttled to a fourth jet, United Airlines Flight 93. According to an account that was on Dewdney's Web site for years, "Passengers filed into the aircraft, urged on by the officials, until the aircraft was full. As it happened, Flight 93 had just enough seats to accommodate the passengers on all four flights." However, Dewdney's calculations are off by a considerable margin. According to Boeing, one of its 757–200ERs can carry 200 people in a standard mixed-class seating configuration. There were 232 passengers on the four doomed jets, plus 33 crew members, for a total of 265 witnesses—a third more than the capacity of the Flight 93 aircraft—all of whom needed to be murdered.

Dewdney's account goes on to claim that Flight 93 was shot down over Shanksville, Pennsylvania, by an A-10 Thunderbolt II that had been painted white, presumably to disguise its military provenance. The three other jets, he speculates, were flown over the Atlantic Ocean and scuttled. According to Dewdney's site, "It is probably the best available description of what probably took place on September 11, 2001."

The theory is an advancement of the "Flight of the Bumble Planes," a hypothesis that first appeared in March 2002 on a Web site at www.public-action.com, which also promotes revisionist histories of the Holocaust. The person who supposedly exposed the plot writes under the pseudonym Snake Plissken, the name of Kurt Russell's character in the science-fiction films *Escape from New York* and *Escape from L.A.*

Not all the theories concerning 9/11 aircraft are as intricate as Dewdney and Plissken's—or require such a large cast of ruthless, tight-lipped conspirators. But all rest on the same small set of factual claims or assumptions.

# The Hijackers' Flying Skills

**CLAIM:** A group of men with no professional flight experience could not have navigated three airplanes across hundreds of miles and into building targets with any accuracy. As an unattributed January 2006 article that originally appeared on www.aljazeera. com asks, "How is it possible that Arab students who had never flown an airplane could take a simulator course and then fly jumbo jets with the skill and precision of 'top-gun' pilots?" The article concludes, "It is obvious that this 'evidence' was planted by individuals wishing to direct the blame towards Osama Bin Laden." The Web site is not affiliated with the Al-Jazeera television network (which operates online at www.aljazeera.net), but describes itself as "an independent media organization established in 1992 in London."

American conspiracy theorists have asked similar questions. Actor Charlie Sheen appeared on *The Alex Jones Show*, a radio broadcast out of Austin, Texas, in March 2006 to discuss his skepticism. "It seems to me like 19 amateurs with box cutters taking over four commercial airliners and hitting 75 percent of their targets . . . it raises a lot of questions," Sheen said.

**FACT:** The terrorists were not highly skilled pilots, but on September 11 they did not have to perform what flight-training professionals consider to be the three most difficult aspects of flying: taking off, flying through inclement weather, and landing. Only one hijacker per plane was trained to fly. In each takeover, based on the evidence of passengers' in-flight phone calls, this man most likely sat quietly in his seat until the "muscle hijackers" had gained control of the cockpit. (The term comes from *The 9/11 Commission Report: Final Report of the National Commission on Terrorist Attacks Upon the United States*.) Then the hijacker pilot took over the plane's operation. Box cutters were not used on all four flights, as Sheen asserted; most of the hijackers used knives to kill and injure passengers and crew. American Airlines Flight 77 was the only one on which box cutters were used, along with knives.

The hijacker pilots—Mohamed Atta (American Airlines Flight 11), Marwan al Shehhi (United Airlines Flight 175), Hani Hanjour (American Airlines Flight 77), and Ziad Jarrah (United Airlines Flight 93)—may not have been highly skilled, but they were not complete amateurs. According to the 9/11 Commission's report, Hanjour earned both his private pilot's license and commercial pilot's license in Arizona, training from 1997 through April 1999, apparently before his involvement began with Al Qaeda. He returned home to Saudi Arabia in late April, and subsequently traveled to Afghanistan, where he trained in Al Qaeda's Al Faruq camp. By December 2000 he was back in Arizona for refresher training on small commercial jets and for Boeing 737 simulator training. Although he was repeatedly encouraged to quit because of his subpar English and poor performance, he finished simulator training in March 2001.

The other three pilots came to the United States in 2000 and underwent at least 40 hours of private flight school to receive private pilot's licenses, which permit flights on single-engine planes. "In order to get a pilot's certificate," says Alison Duquette, a spokeswoman for the Federal Aviation Administration (FAA), "students need to demonstrate written aeronautical knowledge, flight proficiency in an actual through-flight, and then be type-rated" for flying a specific kind of aircraft.

Like Hanjour, the other three men had a rocky training process. Atta and Shehhi changed schools repeatedly after flunking flight exams. But they continued training and by the end of 2000 all but Jarrah had logged a minimum of 250 cumulative flight hours and earned FAA commercial pilot's licenses. Jarrah logged at least 40 flight hours and had become a certified private pilot. The three men then enrolled in simulator training for large jets.

In the months before September 11, at least two of the pilots—Hanjour and Jarrah—requested and subsequently took training flights down the Hudson Corridor, a busy, low-altitude path along the Hudson River that passes by the World Trade Center. Hanjour also took a training flight over Washington D.C. And all four pilots flew cross-country as first-class passengers on United Airlines in the early summer of 2001, which would have given them insights into crew procedures and flight routes.

While it's true that none of the hijacker pilots had ever flown a commercial-size airline jet and had logged far fewer than the 1,500 hours required for FAA airline pilot's licenses, they were, in fact, certified pilots. And the equipment they encountered in the Boeing cockpits on September 11 was similar to the simulators they had trained on in the months before the attacks. So, it's not surprising that they operated the planes with some degree of competence. "When they took over the plane, it was already in flight," says Brian Marsh, a flight instructor at Airline Transport Professionals Flight School, which has classes in 25 cities nationwide. "All they had to do was pretty much point and go. It's even easier than driving a car because there are no roads."

As part of their basic flight training, the hijackers were schooled in the use of the flight management systems and autopilot features. The 9/11 Commission reports that Jarrah purchased a portable Global Positioning System (GPS) unit from a pilot shop in Miami—he tried to buy four, but the store had only one in stock. Atta reportedly purchased three more GPS units, and possibly visited the World Trade Center on September 10, 2001, for a final GPS reading. The pilots had only to punch the destination coordinates into the flight management system and steer the planes while looking at the navigation screen, which all four had done countless times in training. According to Marsh, the navigation systems on airplanes are only slightly more complex than the versions in production automobiles. "The navigation system tells you exactly where you are," Marsh says. "They just had to look at the screen." The flight data recorder, or black box, of Flight 77 indicated that Hanjour input autopilot instructions to Reagan National Airport, less than five miles south of the Pentagon. He steered the plane manually for only the final eight minutes of the flight. To date, no other evidence has been made public about whether Hanjour's co-conspirators flew the planes manually or on autopilot.

While the hijackers ultimately reached three of their four targets, phone transcripts and air traffic control records show that the conspirators' flying skills were indeed rudimentary —far from top-gun material. The planes made sharp turns of up to 330 degrees, in the case of Flight 77, and at times dropped precipitously. Conspiracy theorists describe Hanjour's drastic turn as evidence of great flying skill on the part of whomever—certainly not Hanjour, they contend—was at the controls. They ignore that the turn actually occurred five miles southwest of the Pentagon, possibly because the subpar pilot realized he was vastly too high to hit his target.

Passengers and flight attendants on all four planes reported erratic flying. On Flight 175, passenger Peter Hanson called his father: "Passengers are throwing up and getting sick. The plane is making jerky movements." The hijackers also indicated that they didn't know how to work basic controls in the cockpit. On both Flight 11 and Flight 93, they inadvertently made passenger announcements over air traffic control channels instead of the public address system.

Soon after taking the controls, all four hijackers forced their planes to descend rapidly. In the clear conditions of September 11, they were able to fly by sight rather than by instrument (flying by instrument being a much more difficult skill, although three of the four had earned instrument flight rules certification). The pilots were also helped by choosing targets that were easy to identify from a distance—two towers dominating the New York City skyline and a massive, five-sided compound in suburban Washington D.C. It's possible they could have seen these buildings from as far away as 50 miles on that bright early autumn morning. "With something that large, the target is visual," Marsh says. "It's not hard."

At 8:44 a.m., flight attendant Madeline Sweeney reported further jerky, awkward flying on Flight 11. "Something is wrong. We are in a rapid descent . . . we are all over the place." Her manager asked her to look out the window to see if she could determine the plane's location. "We are flying low," Sweeney said. "We are flying very, very low. We are flying way too low. Oh my God, we are way too low."

Two minutes later, the flight crashed into the North Tower of the World Trade Center.

# Where's the Pod?

**CLAIM:** Photographs and video footage shot just before Flight 175 hit the South Tower of the World Trade Center (WTC 2) seem to show an object underneath the fuselage at the base of the right wing. The documentary film *911 In Plane Site* and the Web site www.letsroll911.org (now www.letsrollforums.com) say that no such object is found on a stock Boeing 767–200ER. This "military pod"—possibly a bomb, a missile, or a piece of equipment from an air-refueling tanker—led www. letsroll911.org to conclude in January 2005 that the attacks were an "inside job" sanctioned by "President George Bush, who planned and engineered 9/11."

**FACT:** The anomalies in the images of Flight can be partially explained by physics: The plane was severely banked when it hit the South Tower. If the airplane had been flying parallel to the ground, it would have hit approximately four stories of the building. Instead, the airplane struck the 77th to 85th floors on impact, destroying nine floors. The *World Trade Center Building Performance Study: Data Collection, Preliminary Observations, and Recommendations*, conducted by the Federal Emergency Management Agency (FEMA), states that Flight 175 hit the building with the left wing at a downward angle of approximately 38 degrees. In addition, Flight 175 approached the tower not head-on, but at a lateral angle of approximately 15 degrees clockwise of the tower's south wall.

As a result, images taken from below or to the side of the South Tower should indeed show a distortion of the right wing in comparison to the left. The effect would be similar to taking a photograph from below of a windmill at different moments in its rotation—depending on the angle of the arms, one arm would look longer and differently proportioned than the other.

One of the clearest, most widely seen pictures of the doomed jet's undercarriage was taken by photographer Rob Howard and published in *New York* magazine and elsewhere (see photo 1). *Popular Mechanics* sent a digital scan of the original photo to Ronald Greeley, director of the Space Photography Laboratory at Arizona State University, in Tempe. Greeley, who has served on a number of NASA committees, is an expert at analyzing images to determine the shape and features of geological formations based on shadow and light effects. After studying the high-resolution image and comparing it to photos of a Boeing 767–200ER's undercarriage, Greeley dismissed the notion that the Howard photo reveals a "pod." In fact, Greeley confirms the photo reveals only the Boeing's right fairing, a pronounced bulge that contains the landing gear. "I conclude," he writes in an e-mail to *Popular Mechanics*, "that it is an artifact of lighting caused by the geometry of the aircraft and the angle of the sun and camera, causing the feature to result from sun glint. Such a glint causes a blossoming (enlargement) on film, which tends to be amplified in digital versions of images—the pixels are saturated and tend to 'spill over' to adjacent pixels."

Thomas R. Edwards, cofounder of TREC, a Huntsville, Alabama, company that analyzes images for law-enforcement agencies, reviewed several images of Flight 175 as presented on conspiracy Web sites and sees further problems. "The images passed around the Web are digital data," Edwards tells *Popular Mechanics*. "You can copy them without loss [of resolution]. But when you take an analog image—the bottom of the barrel, as far as resolution is concerned—and start messing around with it in the digital world by enlarging it or sizing it to fit on a certain page, you have to be very careful with what you are doing." Edwards continues: "Digital magnification by classic techniques gets highly pixilated at times two and beyond. The image just breaks up into squares of meaningless data, with bigger squares as the magnification zooms in closer. The [online] images you view suffer from classic digital magnification. You can draw whatever conclusions you want from a bad photograph."

Edwards, who has testified in two dozen criminal cases, says his role in court is to evaluate the quality of images, not question another person's perception of what the image conveys. But, when pressed for an opinion about whether the photos of Flight 175 show a pod, he responds: "You've got a similar situation here to the folks who think there are UFOs out in Nevada—they have photographs to substantiate their claims. Some of [the images] even look like flying saucers. The bulge on the belly of the plane is an even harder story to swallow. You wouldn't want to go to court with this, I'll tell you that."

The discussion of glints and bulges also overlooks a key fact: Thousands of horrified onlookers saw Flight 175 hit the South Tower; many of them were standing directly under the plane's path. *Popular Mechanics* has been unable to find a single eyewitness account of missiles or ordnance attached to the aircraft.

Photographs aside, military and aviation experts say it is next to impossible to retrofit a passenger plane to carry weapons. "Whoever came up with that has no idea how these things work," says Fred E. C. Culick, professor of aeronautics at the California Institute of Technology. "You have to have the means for setting it off, releasing, and arming it. There are all kinds of little systems involved, [such as] connecting the mounting to the pilot. It would require a lot of metalwork and wiring and, I mean, it's just harebrained. It's not like throwing an extra suitcase in the car."

Finally, as part of a three-year investigation into the collapse of the World Trade Center towers, the National Institute of Standards and Technology (NIST), a nonregulatory agency within the U.S. Department of Commerce, ran computer simulations of the crashes and concluded the damages were consistent with the impacts of airplanes—not missiles or bombs.

# Flight 175's Windows

**CLAIM:** On September 11, soon after Flight 175 crashed into the South Tower, Fox News broadcast a live phone interview with Marc Birnbach, a freelance videographer who was working for the network at the time. "It definitely did not look like a commercial plane," Birnbach said on the air. "I didn't see any windows on the sides."

The Web site www.911inplanesite.com, which promotes the documentary of the same name, states that "Bernback" saw the plane "crash into the South Tower." Coupled with photographs and videos of Flight 175 that lack the resolution to show windows, Birnbach's statement has fueled one of the most widely referenced 9/11 conspiracy theories—specifically, that the South Tower was struck by a military cargo plane or a fuel tanker.

On the site, the producers of the documentary boast that they interviewed Birnbach after his on-air comments and that he stood behind his account that "the plane had no windows."

**FACT:** Birnbach was at the corner of President and Smith streets in Brooklyn, more than two miles southeast of the World Trade Center, when he briefly saw a plane fly over at a considerable distance. He tells *Popular Mechanics* that he did not actually see the plane strike the South Tower but only heard the explosion. He confirms that he spoke to the producers of the documentary *911 In Plane Site* and told them he did not see any windows. But he adds that he doesn't believe the plane was anything other than a passenger jet, and also that he declined the producers' offer to be interviewed on camera for the film. "I just don't want any involvement with them," Birnbach says. "I don't believe their theory. I think they are completely out of line."

It is not surprising that Birnbach did not see windows as the plane passed over. As noted previously (see "Where's the Pod?") the plane approached lower Manhattan from the south over the Hudson River with its wings banked sharply to the left. This means the windows on the right side of the plane—the ones facing people on the ground in Brooklyn and lower Manhattan—were tilted upward.

But the most direct refutation of the "no windows" theory comes from W. Gene Corley, a licensed structural engineer and vice president at Construction Technology Laboratories, a consulting firm based in Skokie, Illinois. While heading the FEMA probe into the collapse of the towers, Corley and his team collected and photographed aircraft debris on the roof of 5 World Trade Center, a nine-story building on the northeast corner of the site. One of the photos shows a chunk of fuselage that clearly had passenger windows (see photo 2).

"It's . . . from the United Airlines plane that hit Tower 2," Corley tells *Popular Mechanics*. In reviewing crash footage taken by an ABC news crew, Corley was able to track the trajectory of the fragments he studied—including a section of the landing gear and part of an engine—as they tore through the South Tower, exited from the building's north side, and fell from the sky. How does he know the debris came from Flight 175, as opposed to some unidentified aircraft? For one thing, the fragments carried the gray and blue markings of United Airlines planes. "The fuselage fragments were from the rear section of the plane," Corley adds. "One fragment had three windows on it, and there was a fragment that had part of the landing gear. And there was an engine fragment— most of the engine." Some fragments also contained parts numbers that corresponded to components of the 767 used on Flight 175.

# No Stand-Down Order

**CLAIM:** To prevent the military from interfering with deadly attacks planned by the president and his co-conspirators, theorists claim, U.S. armed forces were grounded on September 11; more specifically, no fighter jets were scrambled from any of the 28 Air Force bases within range of the four hijacked flights.

Even in the contentious world of conspiracy theorists, there is near unanimity on this issue: "On 11 September Andrews [Air Force Base] had two squadrons of fighter jets with the job of protecting the skies over Washington D.C.," says the Web site www.emperors-clothes.com. "They failed to do their job."

"There is only one explanation for this," concludes Mark R. Elsis of www.standdown.net. "Our Air Force was ordered to Stand Down on 9/11."

**FACT:**    On September 11, only 14 fighter jets were on alert in the contiguous 48 states. Several jets were scrambled in response to the hijackings, but they were too late to affect the day's terrible outcomes. The delay was caused by a series of communication breakdowns among government officials and an inability to quickly process and react to an unprecedented event.

At the time, no computer network or alarm system was in place to automatically alert the North American Aerospace Defense Command (NORAD) of missing civilian planes. "They [civilian Air Traffic Control, or ATC] had to pick up the phone and literally dial us," says Major Douglas Martin, former public affairs officer for NORAD, in an interview with *Popular Mechanics.*

Under the protocols in place on September 11, a controller's concerns that something was amiss had to ascend through multiple layers at the FAA and the Department of Defense before action could be taken. In the case of a hijacking, a controller would alert his or her supervisor, who contacted another supervisor, who confirmed suspicion of hijacking and informed a series of managers, all the way to the national ATC Command Center in Herndon, Virginia, which then notified FAA headquarters in Washington.

The director of the Office of Civil Aviation Security was the FAA's hijack coordinator. If the director confirmed the incident as a hijacking, he or she would contact the Pentagon to request a military escort aircraft from the National Military Command Center (NMCC), which is located in the Joint Staff area of the Pentagon and is the logistical and communications locus for the National Command Authority (the president and the secretary of defense). The NMCC then would request approval from the office of the secretary of defense. If given, the order for a military escort would be relayed to NORAD, which would then order mission crew commanders at the appropriate air force bases in one of three continental U.S. air defense sectors (there are now two) to scramble fighters. The fighters would then scramble, receive target and vector information while aloft, and follow the hijacked airliner, monitoring its flight path and assisting in search and rescue in the case of an emergency.

According to the detailed account provided in the 9/11 Commission's report, the first alarm was sounded at Boston Center, one of 22 FAA regional ATC facilities, after an air traffic controller received the following transmission at 8:24 a.m. from Flight 11: "We have some planes. Just stay quiet and you'll be okay. We are returning to the airport."

Then, seconds later, came a second transmission: "Nobody move. Everything will be okay. If you try to make any moves, you'll endanger yourself and the airplane. Just stay quiet." Upon hearing the second message, the controller concluded that Flight 11 had been hijacked. He consulted his supervisors; at 8:37 a.m., Boston Center bypassed the prescribed protocol and contacted NORAD's Northeast Air Defense Sector (NEADS). Two F-15s were immediately ordered to battle stations at Otis Air National Guard Base in Falmouth, Massachusetts, 153 miles northeast of New York City. But NEADS did not know where to send the fighters; they sat at Otis for another 16 minutes while controllers struggled to unravel the events unfolding before them.

There are two primary ways controllers keep track of planes in the air: two-way radios and a transponder, which emits an electronic signal that relays the plane's tail number, altitude, and speed. In addition, controllers use ground-based primary radar to scan the skies; the radar signal that bounces off the aircraft shows up as a blip on a radar screen. But without the additional information provided by the transponder, it is difficult for controllers to know which blip represents which particular aircraft. (The difficulty of keeping track of multiple aircraft using ground-based radar alone is one reason the military typically flies sophisticated radar aircraft, known as Airborne Warning and Control Systems, or AWACS, over battle zones.)

One of the first steps the hijackers took after seizing control of the four aircraft was to turn off the jets' transponders. At the time of the hijackings, there were 4,500 planes in the skies over the continental United States. Without transponder data or radio contact, controllers were forced to search for the missing aircraft among all the identical radar blips, with each controller responsible for varying numbers of planes in his or her sector. The Indianapolis controller who first noticed Flight 77's disappearance, for instance, had been monitoring 15 planes. In addition, on September 11, 2001, the ATC systems were woefully inadequate. The Cleveland Air Traffic Control did not even have combined transponder and radar displays: To view primary radar, controllers had to go to displays on a different floor.

At 8:46 a.m., before the F-15s from Otis Air Force Base were even airborne, Flight 11 smashed into the North Tower of the World Trade Center. The fighters took off just before

8:53 a.m. on a preassigned vector, per standard operating procedure. In this case, they were sent to military airspace off Long Island, New York, to await target assignment.

Meanwhile, Flight 175 had also been hijacked, but the New York Air Traffic Control was slow to respond, in part because the controller assigned to the flight was also assigned to Flight 11 and was busy searching for that missing plane amid news reports that an aircraft had just hit the North Tower. At 9:03 a.m., at almost the exact moment Flight 175 hit the South Tower, the New York Center called NEADS directly to report that Flight 175 had been hijacked—an event some NEADS personnel were watching live on TV. The fighters awaiting target assignments off Long Island did not know that a second hijacked plane was en route to New York City. Within five minutes of the second plane's impact, the NEADS mission crew commander asked for authorization to station the fighters over Manhattan in case there were even more hijacked planes. At 9:25 a.m., the two fighters established combat air patrol over the city.

The confusion over Flight 77 was arguably more pronounced. When the plane's transponder was shut off and radio calls went unreturned, the FAA's Indianapolis Center believed the aircraft had crashed; the controller there was not yet aware of the other hijacked planes. The controller tracking the plane tried in vain to find it on its scheduled flight plan to the west, unaware that it had turned back east. Flight 77 flew undetected toward Washington for 36 minutes.

At 9:09 a.m., NEADS contacted Langley Air Force Base in Hampton, Virginia, and asked for additional fighters to be placed at battle stations. This was a cautionary measure to ensure that other fighters could be scrambled quickly if the Otis-based jets ran short on fuel. At 9:30 a.m., two Langley F-16s took off, although the pilots mistakenly believed they were on the lookout for Flight 11, unaware that it had already crashed into the World Trade Center; they also did not know Flight 77 was missing.

At 9:32 a.m., controllers at Washington Dulles International Airport spotted an inbound plane and relayed the information to the Secret Service. No one notified NEADS—and the fighters headed east over the Atlantic Ocean, in part because of a generic flight plan designed to get fighters at Langley airborne and out of the crowded local airspace as quickly as possible to prevent collisions. Once controllers at Boston Center realized that an unidentified aircraft was closing in on Washington, the F-16s were ordered to return to the D.C. area at top speed. "I don't care how many windows you break," the commander told the pilots, authorizing them to fly at supersonic speeds, contrary to existing military procedure and NORAD and FAA regulations for civilian U.S. airspace. The fighters were still 150 miles east of the capital when Flight 77 hit the Pentagon at 9:37 a.m.

At 9:32 a.m. the FAA's Cleveland Center received a transmission from one of the hijackers on Flight 93: "Keep remaining sitting. We have a bomb on board." It was one of the inadvertent passenger announcements the hijackers made over air traffic control channels. Nine minutes later, the center lost the plane's transponder signal. Indecisiveness at the ATC Command Center, in Herndon, and at FAA headquarters in Washington D.C., delayed a request for military assistance. According to the 9/11 Commission's report,

"NORAD did not even know the plane was hijacked until after it had crashed" in a field near Shanksville, in southwestern Pennsylvania.

The earliest written confirmation of President Bush's shoot-down order for any hijacked plane headed toward the capital came at 10:20 a.m. when White House press secretary Ari Fleischer, on Air Force One, recorded that the president had issued the directive. That was a full 17 minutes after Flight 93's demise concluded the morning's grisly chain of events. The time from the notification of the first hijacking to the crash of Flight 93 was 104 minutes.

It seems unbelievable to many conspiracy theorists that between the FAA and NORAD, the government could not find the hijacked flights or identify them earlier as threats that needed to be addressed militarily. But, as noted, the terrorists thwarted the FAA by turning off the transponders and not responding to radio transmissions. As for NORAD's more sophisticated radar, it ringed the continent, looking outward for threats, not inward.

"When you looked at NORAD on September 11, we had a ring of radar all around both [Canada and the United States]," Martin says. "It was like a donut. There was no coverage in the middle. That was not the threat."

Equally unprecedented was a virtually silent hijacking, where no attempts were made, by either the airline pilots or the hijackers, to alert the authorities to the specifics of the situation. Without direct communication from either the pilots or the hijackers, the FAA, for the first time in its history, had to guess how to respond. "Controllers were forced to take action based on what we knew at the time, and there was no precedent or specific procedure for dealing with that situation," says FAA spokeswoman Laura Brown.

"You have to realize that prior to 9/11, all of the hijackings that happened anywhere in the world never ended in what we saw on that day," Chris Yates tells *Popular Mechanics*. Yates is the aviation security editor and analyst for *Jane's Defence Weekly*, which covers the military industry. Under the hijacking scenarios that U.S. civilian and military officials had prepared for, Yates says, "the hijackers were making a political statement, they were making a bunch of demands, eventually the aircraft would land somewhere, and either the powers . . . in that jurisdiction acquiesced to the demands of the hijackers, or it resulted in a standoff for $x$ number of days."

Further, even if the FAA had decided within the first minutes of Flight 11's erratic behavior and loss of communication that a hijacking had taken place and alerted the military, NORAD's rules of engagement did not permit fighter pilots to shoot down commercial aircraft. "A hijack in the United States or Canada today would immediately be considered the act of a terrorist and an act of war," Martin says. "On September 11 it was not; it was a criminal act."

What about Andrews Air Force Base, which is just 10 miles southeast of the Pentagon? As the base nearest the nation's capital, didn't it have fighters on constant alert? The answer is no. "There was no reason to—and that's a key point here," Yates says. "The U.S. homeland had never been attacked previously in this way—apart from Pearl Harbor."

According to Staff Sergeant Sean McEntee, public affairs specialist for the 113th Wing of the District of Columbia Air National Guard, the fighter jets based at Andrews are now part of the Department of Homeland Security's Operation Noble Eagle. "The job of the F-16s is to control the airspace around the capital," McEntee says. "They are only for national capital emergencies. The operation was set up after 9/11. It didn't exist at the time."

The 9/11 Commission's report adds: "In sum, the protocols in place on 9/11 for the FAA and NORAD to respond to a hijacking presumed that the hijacked aircraft would be readily identifiable and would not attempt to disappear; there would be time to address the problem through the appropriate FAA and NORAD chains of command; and the hijacking would take the traditional form: That is, it would not be a suicide hijacking designed to convert the aircraft into a guided missile. On the morning of 9/11, the existing protocol was unsuited in every respect for what was about to happen."

# Military Intercepts

**CLAIM:** The military should have been able to intercept several, if not all, of the hijacked planes because military pilots regularly fly similar missions. "It has been standard operating procedures for decades to immediately intercept off-course planes that do not respond to communications from air traffic controllers," says the Web site www.oilempire.us. "When the Air Force 'scrambles' a fighter plane to intercept, they usually reach the plane in question in minutes."

In his book, *The New Pearl Harbor: Disturbing Questions About the Bush Administration and 9/11*, retired theology professor David Ray Griffin cites a September 15, 2001, *Boston Globe* article in which a NORAD spokesman was paraphrased as saying essentially the same thing: The agency's fighters routinely intercept aircraft.

**FACT:** In the decade before 9/11, NORAD intercepted only one civilian plane over North America: golfer Payne Stewart's Learjet in October 1999. Stewart and five others were flying from Orlando, Florida, to Dallas when the plane lost cabin pressure at approximately 39,000 feet. With passengers and crew unconscious from cabin decompression, the plane crashed four hours later in a field near Aberdeen, South Dakota.

Some conspiracy theorists mistakenly believe the Stewart case bolsters their argument that fighters can reach wayward passenger planes within minutes, as controllers lost contact with the plane around 9:33 a.m. and an F-16 from Eglin Air Force Base in Fort Walton Beach, Florida, intercepted it at 9:52 a.m. But they overlook an important detail in the accident report from the National Transportation Safety Board: The plane was lost at 9:33 eastern daylight time and intercepted at 9:52 central daylight time, making the total time 1 hour and 19 minutes for the fighter to reach the stricken jet.

The F-16 was already in the air on a training run and did not have to be scrambled to pursue the Learjet. It did have to refuel, however, so the actual time it took for the F-16 to chase down the Learjet was about 50 minutes. One reason it took so long: Rules in effect prior to 9/11, which have since been rescinded, prohibited supersonic flight on intercepts.

Another important point about the Stewart incident: The Learjet's transponder was active, making identification and tracking straightforward. The fighters that were scrambled on 9/11 did not have such clear-cut targets, as the transponders on the hijacked airliners were turned off. Besides, even if one of the fighters had located a hijacked plane, what could the pilot have done? As noted previously (see "No Stand-Down Order") the authorization to shoot down civilian airliners was not given until after the fourth plane had crashed.

But what about the *Boston Globe* report, in which the NORAD spokesman said that intercepts were routine? When contacted by *Popular Mechanics*, spokesmen for NORAD and the FAA clarified their remarks by noting that scrambles were routine, but intercepts were not—especially over the continental United States. A *scramble* is when pilots are rushed to their aircraft from the ground for takeoff, whereas an *intercept* is an actual midair approach to another plane. (Note: The numbers do not always match up, as some intercepts can be *diverts,* whereby a plane already in the air intercepts the target, as in the Payne Stewart incident, where there was an intercept but not a scramble.)

Many conspiracy theorists cite an August 12, 2002, Associated Press story as "proof" that NORAD mounted more frequent interceptions of domestic flights. The article paraphrased Martin: "From September 11 to June [2002], NORAD scrambled jets or diverted combat air patrols 462 times, almost seven times as often as the 67 scrambles from September 2000 to June 2001." However, the Knight-Ridder/ Tribune News Service produced a more complete account, which included an important qualification. Here's how the

Knight-Ridder story appeared in the September 28, 2002, edition of the *Colorado Springs Gazette:* "From June 2000 to September 2001, NORAD scrambled fighters 67 times *but not over the continental United States."* (Emphasis added.) Some conspiracy theorists also ignore the following passage from the same article: "Before September 11, the only time officials recall scrambling jets over the United States was when golfer Payne Stewart's plane veered off course and crashed in South Dakota in 1999."

Except for that lone, tragic anomaly, all NORAD interceptions from the end of the Cold War in 1989 until 9/11 took place in offshore Air Defense Identification Zones (ADIZ), which require that planes flying through file flight plans and have transponders and two-way radios. The planes intercepted in these zones were primarily being used for drug smuggling. "Until 9/11 there was no domestic ADIZ," says FAA spokesman Bill Schumann.

After 9/11, the FAA and NORAD increased cooperation, setting up hotlines between air traffic control centers and NORAD command centers and establishing an ADIZ zone over Washington D.C. Moreover, NORAD has increased its fighter coverage and installed additional radar to monitor airspace over the continent.

"From September 11, 2000, to October 10, 2000, we had, in all of NORAD, seven scrambles," Martin says. "Six were training. In the same period, a year later, from September 11, 2001, to October 10, 2001, we had 86 scrambles or diversions of air patrols. So, 86 times more, because of threats."

In the same *Boston Globe* article cited by Griffin, former U.S. Senator Warren Rudman (Republican from New

Hampshire) gave a more accurate assessment of the military's pre-9/11 intercept capabilities. "This country is not on a wartime footing," said Rudman, who served as cochairman of the U.S. Commission on National Security in 2001. "We don't have capable fighter aircraft loaded with missiles sitting on runways in this country. We just don't do that anymore. We did back during the '70s, the '60s, along the coast, being concerned about Russian intrusion, but to expect American fighter aircraft to intercept commercial airliners, who knows where, is totally unrealistic and makes no sense at all."

# 2

# WORLD TRADE CENTER TOWERS 1 & 2

On July 28, 1945, a B-25 bomber flying through foggy skies at 200 miles per hour plowed into the 79th floor of the Empire State Building in midtown Manhattan. One of the plane's engines penetrated the opposite side of the building and crashed through a nearby roof. Nearly 800 gallons of high-octane fuel exploded upon impact and ignited a series of fires inside the building.

The similarities between that event and the attacks on the World Trade Center a half century later are striking. There is, of course, an obvious difference: The Empire State Building, which opened in 1931, suffered little serious damage outside the immediate areas of impact. Only 14 people, including the bomber's pilot and two others on board the plane, were killed.

If the older Empire State Building could withstand such a blow, why not the Twin Towers? Conspiracy theorists insist on a different answer: The buildings were brought down intentionally—not by hijacked airplanes, but by government-planted bombs or a controlled demolition.

In an online essay, Danish writer Henrik Melvang declares, "Both the WTC Twintowers [sic] were exposed to heavy bombs being detonated inside and below—before the Towers fell down." Melvang thinks that bombings were part of a wide-ranging plot by the Freemasons to create a New World Order. On his Web site www.bombsinsidewtc. dk, Melvang also markets his book and video claiming the Apollo moon landings were a hoax.

Not everyone inclined to believe that bombs were used to bring down the towers is so far removed from the mainstream. Morgan Reynolds, a former chief economist at the U.S. Department of Labor, concludes that "only professional demolition appears to account for the full range of facts associated with the collapse of the three buildings." Reynolds is a professor emeritus in the economics department at Texas A&M University and a member of Scholars for 9/11 Truth, a group of academics and others "dedicated to exposing falsehoods and to revealing truths behind 9/11." After Reynolds made his views public, Texas A&M president Robert Gates released a statement noting that Reynolds did not keep an office on the campus and characterizing the professor's comments as "beyond the pale." (Conspiracy theorists have an explanation for the presidential rebuke: Gates formerly served as head of the CIA.)

Though Reynolds and a handful of other skeptics cite academic credentials to lend credence to their views, not one of the leading conspiracy theorists has a background in engineering, construction, or related fields. In fact, the collapses of the three World Trade Center buildings are among the most extensively studied structural failures in American history. In the five years since 9/11, they have been the subject of lengthy investigations and engineering school symposiums, together involving hundreds of experts from academia and private industry, as well as the government. The conclusions reached by these experts have been consistent: A combination of physical damage from the airplane crashes and prolonged exposure to the resulting fires ultimately destroyed the structural integrity of all three buildings.

# The Empire State Building Accident

**CLAIM:** Some conspiracy theorists point to the bomber crashing into the Empire State Building as proof that commercial planes hitting the World Trade Center could not bring down the towers. "It may be 'obvious' that a heavy plane hitting a skyscraper would deliver a 'tremendous' shock," claims www.serendipity.li, a Web site operated by computer programmer Peter Meyer, "but it doesn't follow that the building must therefore collapse. In 1945 the Empire State Building was hit by a B-25 bomber, but it was still standing last time I saw it." The site describes itself as "opposed to Fascism, Zionism, Capitalism, the New World Order, and all those who secretly work to cause wars for their own advantage."

**FACT:** Like most skyscrapers built prior to the 1960s, the Empire State Building was stiffly constructed with reinforced-concrete columns and a thick masonry exterior. "The Empire State Building is 38 pounds per cubic foot," says Vincent Dunn, former New York deputy fire chief and author of *The Collapse of Burning Buildings.* "It's the ultimate concrete high-rise building—the ultimately stable high-rise."

The World Trade Center towers, which opened in 1970, marked a significant departure in terms of design that greatly affected the way the buildings reacted to the airplane crashes. The towers were tubular structures in which a dense interior core of steel and concrete—where elevators, stairwells, and bathrooms were located—shared load-bearing responsibilities with a relatively thin exterior shell of 14-inch-square box columns fabricated from steel plates. The floors were supported with lightweight strips of steel called *trusses.* A densely woven set of trusses, known collectively as a *hat truss,* sat atop the structures to further help distribute loads. The design marked a commercial advance, as the absence of interior columns allowed for nearly 40,000 square feet of office space per floor. But it also created structures that were in some ways more fragile. "If you look at a modern high-rise building, it has a density of around eight to nine pounds per cubic foot. That's lighter than balsa wood, which is 10 pounds per cubic foot. These structures look massive, but they're mostly air. They *are* air, punctuated with thin layers of concrete and steel," says Jon Magnusson, CEO of Magnusson Klemencic Associates, an engineering firm based in Seattle, Washington. One of the firm's founders was the late John Skilling, one of two structural engineers primarily responsible for the design of the towers. "The World Trade Center [towers]," Dunn adds, "[were] the ultimate lightweight high-rise buildings."

Leslie Robertson, Skilling's chief colleague in the WTC project, told the *New Yorker* magazine in a November 2001 article that he and Skilling engineered the towers to withstand the impact of a Boeing 707, the largest commercial airliner at the time. "We studied it, and designed for the impact of such an aircraft," Robertson said. "The next step would have been to think about the fuel load, and I've been searching my brain, but I don't know what happened there, whether in all our testing we thought about it. Now we know what happens—it explodes. I don't know if we considered the fire damage that would cause."

Robertson, whose office was blocks from Ground Zero, was racked with grief after 9/11. "The World Trade Center was a team effort," he told the *New Yorker*, "but the collapse of the World Trade Center is my responsibility, and that's the way I feel about it."

Many structural engineers feel differently, saying that the design of the Twin Towers enabled the structures to stand as long as they did, which helped save thousands of lives. "Ninety-nine percent of all [modern] high-rises, if hit with a large-scale commercial aircraft, would collapse immediately," Magnusson tells *Popular Mechanics*. "Not just collapse, but collapse immediately."

In his book, *Why Buildings Fall Down: How Structures Fail*, structural engineer Matthys Levy notes that when the bomber struck the Empire State Building, it punched an 18-by 20-foot hole in the exterior but did not critically damage any load-bearing columns. He says there were key differences between that incident and the 9/11 attacks, in addition to the Empire State Building's massively over-built concrete-clad steel frame and masonry exterior: The bomber was going only 200 miles per hour, compared to more than 440 and 540 miles per hour for the planes that hit the North and South towers, respectively; the bomber was less than one-tenth the weight of the 767s that hit the towers and carried only one-tenth as much fuel; the bomber's wings were flat instead of banked and therefore hit just the 79th floor rather than multiple floors; and the bomber's fuselage hit just to the right of a major column instead of shearing multiple load-bearing columns.

# Widespread Damage

**CLAIM:** The first hijacked plane crashed through the 93rd to the 99th floors of the World Trade Center's 110-story North Tower; the second jet slammed into the 77th to the 85th floors of the 110-story South Tower. The impact and ensuing fires disrupted elevator service and caused significant damage to the lobbies in both buildings before they collapsed, which strikes some as suspicious. "There is NO WAY the impact of the jet caused such widespread damage eighty stories below," claims a posting on the San Diego Independent Media Center Web site at www. sandiego.indymedia.org. "It is OBVIOUS and irrefutable that OTHER EXPLOSIVES ( . . . such as concussion bombs) HAD ALREADY BEEN DETONATED in the lower levels of tower one at the same time as the plane crash."

**FACT:** A three-year study into the collapse of the towers found that plane debris sliced through the utility shafts in both towers' cores, creating conduits for burning jet fuel—and fiery destruction throughout the buildings.

Following up on a May 2002 preliminary report by the Federal Emergency Management Agency (FEMA), the National Institute of Standards and Technology (NIST), a branch of the U.S. Department of Commerce, released the *Final Report of the National Construction Safety Team on the Collapses of the World Trade Center* in September 2005. Though often derided by conspiracy theorists as the "government version," the 10,000-page NIST report included the input of hundreds of experts from private industry and academia. A supplement to the report notes that "elevator lobbies throughout the building were particularly affected [by the airplane impacts], likely by excess jet fuel ignited by the crash pouring down the elevator shafts."

NIST lead investigator Shyam Sunder explains that the burning jet fuel simply followed the path of least resistance. "The core of the building is where a large number of elevator shafts and stairwells were damaged. These provided an easy path for jet fuel to traverse down," Sunder tells *Popular Mechanics.*

NIST investigators spoke with more than 1,000 survivors and witnesses of the attack as part of their attempt to determine the progression of damage to the buildings. A number of witnesses reported seeing pockets of fire in locations far from floors directly affected by the aircraft impacts. One survivor—NIST granted all witnesses anonymity in exchange for their cooperation—near an elevator between the 40th and 50th floors of the North Tower recalled, "I saw the elevator in front of me had flames coming out of it. The elevator was closed but the flames came from the front where the doors meet and on the sides. . . . I saw a chandelier shaking; it was really moving. . . . Black smoke started filling the corridor, it got really dense, really fast." And a survivor in the basement of the North Tower at the time of the attack recalled, "I saw a big bright orange color coming through the basement with the smoke. . . . A fireball came shooting out of the basement door."

Investigators heard additional reports that "some elevators slammed right down" to the ground floor in loud, violent crashes. "The doors cracked open on the lobby floor and flames came out and people died," says James Quintiere, an engineering professor at the University of Maryland and a NIST adviser. A similar observation was made in the film *9/11*, by Jules and Gedeon Naudet. On the day of the attacks, the French brothers were making a documentary about Tony Benetatos, a rookie New York City firefighter with an engine and ladder company on Duane Street, a few blocks from the World Trade Center. Some of those firefighters became the first responders to the North Tower. As Jules Naudet followed them into the lobby, minutes after the first aircraft struck, the filmmaker saw victims on fire, a scene he found too horrific to record.

The Empire State Building accident in 1945 also generated damage far from the impact area. Structural engineer Levy notes that when the B-25 struck the Manhattan landmark, the plane's fuel plummeted down the elevator shafts and caused fire damage in the lobby (see photo 19). "The two incidents certainly are similar" in that respect, Levy tells *Popular Mechanics*. "Where else is the fuel going to go? It spreads across the floor, and whenever there's a vertical shaft, it goes down."

The fuel in the core of the World Trade Center towers was not the only cause of disturbances on the lower floors. The violent swaying of the buildings following the crashes also caused severe damage. "The vigorous shaking of the building associated with the impact was enough to cause what we call secondary damage," Sunder says. "In this case, we had extensive damage to ceiling tiles, walls, and partitions throughout the building."

As for those who believe bombs may have been planted in the buildings, one of the primary sources they cite is New York City firefighter Louie Cacchioli. Shortly after Cacchioli led 40 office workers out of the North Tower, the South Tower collapsed, enveloping him in a cloud of debris he thought would kill him. A *People* magazine reporter approached Cacchioli shortly after he was pulled out of the wreckage. "On the last trip up, a bomb went off," he said in the resulting article. "We think there was [sic] bombs set in the building."

A 20-year department veteran whose photograph is on the cover of the Time-Life book, *Faces of Ground Zero*, Cacchioli is seemingly an unimpeachable source. Several conspiracy sites reported contacting Cacchioli and stated that he stood by his story. On the Web site www.911truth.org, David Ray Griffin, author of the book *The New Pearl Harbor*, reported that Cacchioli attempted to tell his story to the 9/11 Commission. "They were trying to twist my words and make the story fit only what they wanted to hear," Griffin quotes Cacchioli as saying. "All I wanted to do was tell the truth and when they wouldn't let me do that, I walked out."

According to Cacchioli, it is the conspiracy theorists who are twisting his words. "That was a misquote," he tells *Popular Mechanics*, referring to the initial comment about believing there were bombs in the building. "It was in *People* magazine. They interviewed me when they finally got me out of the rubble. I said, 'It sounded like a bomb.' I tried to explain what I meant [after the fact] but it was already out there."

Cacchioli, who retired from the fire department for health reasons originating on September 11, says he has been contacted repeatedly by people hoping he will say that there were bombs in the building, but he refuses to do so. In addition, he says he walked out of the interview with the 9/11 Commission in anger after a discussion about the effectiveness of the radios and the evacuation order on September 11—not because he raised the issue of bombs.

Cacchioli, like every other firefighter contacted by *Popular Mechanics*, accepts that the combination of jet impacts and fire brought down the WTC buildings. He also tells *Popular Mechanics* that he feels misrepresented by the media, and is distressed at the inaccurate use of his name in conjunction with conspiracy theories.

# Melted Steel

**CLAIM:** The mainstream account of the collapse of the Twin Towers asserts that the plane crashes ignited a series of blazes that weakened the steel columns until they eventually gave way and collapsed. Conspiracy theorists argue that this is implausible, if not impossible. "We have been lied to," announces the Web site www. attackonamerica.net. "The first lie was that the load of fuel from the aircraft was the cause of structural failure. No kerosene fire can burn hot enough to melt steel." The posting is titled "Proof Of Controlled Demolition At The WTC." In support of this view, many theorists point to the initial FEMA report, which acknowledges that no large fire-protected steel-frame building had previously collapsed solely due to fire.

Brigham Young University physicist Steven E. Jones takes the argument one step further. In a paper he published online—*Why Indeed did the World Trade Center Buildings Completely Collapse on 9-11-01?*—Jones asks: "The government reports admit that the building fires were insufficient to melt steel beams—then where did the molten metal pools come from?" According to his theory, the only logical explanation is that the buildings were brought down with explosives.

**FACT:** At the time of impact, the planes were each carrying around 10,000 gallons of jet fuel. Jet fuel burns at 1,100 to 1,200 degrees Celsius (2,012 to 2,190 degrees Fahrenheit), significantly less than the 1,510 degrees Celsius (2,750 degrees Fahrenheit) typically required to melt steel. However, experts agree that for the towers to collapse, their steel frames didn't need to melt, they just had to lose some of their structural strength—and that required exposure to much less heat.

According to NIST's final report, the two towers collapsed in similar but slightly different modes. When the planes hit the buildings and plowed into their centers, a large section of the exterior load-bearing columns as well as some crucial core columns were severed. This transferred additional loads to the surviving columns. NIST believes a great deal of the fireproofing insulation was likely knocked off the surviving columns in the impact, leaving them more vulnerable to the heat. In WTC 2, for instance, NIST found that the impact stripped fireproofing insulation from trusses that supported 80,000 square feet of floor space. The spray-on fireproofing, which was first used widely in the 1960s, is lightweight and fluffy and can crumble from the touch of a hand, much less the impact of plane debris flying at several hundred miles per hour. In addition, the remaining fireproofing can trap heat that reaches the steel in exposed areas, magnifying the effect of that heat.

And jet fuel wasn't the only thing burning, notes Forman Williams, a professor of engineering at the University of California, San Diego. He says that while the jet fuel was the catalyst for the WTC fires, the resulting infernos were intensified by the combustible material inside the buildings, including rugs, curtains, furniture, and paper.

"The jet fuel was the ignition source," Williams tells *Popular Mechanics.* "It burned for maybe 10 minutes, and [the towers] were still standing in 10 minutes. It was the rest of the stuff burning afterward that was responsible for the heat transfer that eventually brought [the towers] down."

The NIST report states that pockets of air hit 1,000 degrees Celsius (1,832 Fahrenheit). Steel begins to lose strength at temperatures as low as about 400 degrees Celsius (750 Fahrenheit) and loses roughly 50 percent of its strength at approximately 600 degrees Celsius (1,100 Fahrenheit). At

980 degrees Celsius (1,800 Fahrenheit), it retains less than 10 percent, says Farid Alfawakhiri, the senior engineer of construction codes and standards at the American Iron and Steel Institute, an industry group in Washington D.C.

The Twin Tower fires were unlike previous high-rise fires: A typical office fire starts at a single location and spreads, consuming fuel as it goes. By the time the fire reaches more distant locations, the combustibles at its starting point have been largely consumed and temperatures in that area begin to drop. But the planes that struck the two towers involved multiple floors, slicing through floors 93 to 99 in the North Tower and 77 to 85 in the South Tower. Those impacts tore through flimsy interior walls and splashed fuel over large areas. The resulting conflagrations were immediate and widespread.

As the fires blazed and the temperatures rose within the buildings, NIST believes, the remaining core columns softened and buckled, transferring most of the load to the building's outer structural columns. The floors outside the impact zone, which are believed to have remained intact, began to sag from the heat, pulling those columns inward and adding to the burden on the outer columns.

In the North Tower, the exterior columns then began to bow inward and buckle. The buckling columns finally surpassed the strain that could be absorbed, initiating a global collapse. In the South Tower, the floors appear to have played a larger role. Fires caused them to sag as much as two feet, adding to the inward pull that had already been initiated by the buckling of the central columns. In both cases, the final result was collapse.

Conspiracy theorists point to other high-rise fires, such as the one in 1991 at the 38-story Meridian Plaza hotel in Philadelphia, as proof that fire alone cannot bring down a skyscraper. And, in a sense, they are right: Fire alone did not bring down the towers.

"If the buildings had not been damaged by airplanes, they could have lost strength and still stood," says structural engineer Magnusson. "But the airplanes did two things in terms of the buildings' survivability: First, they damaged the structure, so they took out the towers' redundancy, their ability to balance overload. The structure load went way up. Then, the impact struck out sprinklers and fireproofing, and the fire elevated the temperature of steel. Then you start to weaken the steel by heating it up. And it was only those two things in combination that were enough to bring the buildings down."

In his paper, BYU's Jones raises a separate series of steel-related questions, all of which he says point to the conclusion that the towers were brought down by explosives. He argues, for example, that the presence of molten metal contradicts the NIST finding that the fires never reached temperatures high enough to melt steel.

But three experts who support the mainstream account of the towers' collapse tell *Popular Mechanics* that the issue is a red herring. They note that the debris pile sat cooking for weeks, with the materials at the bottom of the pile getting increasingly hot because the fires were confined and lost minimal heat to the atmosphere. As a result, the fires could have easily reached temperatures sufficient to melt steel, not to mention most of the other metals found in the buildings. (A

November 19, 2001, article in the *New York Times* reported that the fires were still burning more than two months after the tower collapses and that firefighting experts were calling it the longest-burning commercial building fire ever recorded.) "When we're talking about the debris pile and the insulating effect, the fires down there are completely different than the factors [affecting the steel] in the building," Magnusson says. "That in and of itself is nowhere near the physical evidence that there must have been explosives. That's a leap."

Two metallurgy professors also say they found flaws with the evidence Jones uses to support his arguments. According to Alan Pense, professor emeritus of metallurgical engineering at Lehigh University, "The photographs shown to support melting steel are, to me, either unconvincing . . . or show materials that appear to be other than steel. One of these photos appears to me to be mostly of glass with unmelted steel rods in it. Glass melts at much lower temperatures than steel."

Elsewhere in the paper, Jones claims the molten metal could have been caused by cutter charges like "HMX, or RDX, or some combination thereof, routinely used to melt/cut/demolish steel."

But, Mark Loizeaux, president of Controlled Demolition Inc., says Jones misunderstands the properties of explosive charges. Although these charges provide intense heat, he says, the velocity of detonation is too fast—28,000 feet per second—to melt steel. When an explosive is detonated, it cuts through steel with force; it does not burn through it with heat. He makes the analogy of a person putting his hand through a candle: He can swipe it straight through the flame quickly without getting burned. But if he holds it several inches above the flame for an extended period, he will get burned. "The difference is the duration of exposure," he says. "I can put a shaped charge on a steel column for a test shot and then walk right up and put my hand on the column. There's no heat [because it burns too fast]. Now, how do they make steel in a steel mill? They take fuel and they keep heating the iron ore or scrap steel until it melts. So, could explosives melt steel? Absolutely not. It's too fast an exposure."

# Free-Fall Times

**CLAIM:** One relatively recent conspiracy theory about the Twin Towers involves the time it took each building to collapse. The only way these structures could have fallen at near-free-fall speeds, conspiracists say, is if all internal resistance had been blown away as the towers collapsed, via controlled demolition. "If [the official story is to be believed], the lower floors, with all their steel and concrete, would have provided resistance," David Ray Griffin writes at www.911review.com. "The upper floors could not have fallen through them at the same speed as they would fall through air. However, the videos of the collapses show that the rubble falling inside the building's profile falls at the same speed as the rubble outside." Rosie O'Donnell clarified the position while cohosting *The View*: "Do you know how fast it took those towers to fall? Nine seconds," she said. "You know how fast it would have taken something to free-fall from the top of that building? Nine seconds. It's physically impossible."

There remains reasonable scholarly debate as to how fast the towers actually fell. Eduardo Kausel, an MIT professor of civil and environmental engineering, has estimated the collapses at about nine seconds apiece. The 9-11 Commission's report says, "At 9:58:59, the South Tower (WTC 2) collapsed in ten seconds." Even conspiracists can't agree on times. Some, like O'Donnell, focus on the nine-second estimate, but www.911review.com says, "Each of the Twin Towers totally collapsed in intervals of approximately 14 to 16 seconds." Andrew Johnson, part of the West Yorkshire Truth Campaign (wytruth.org.uk), repeats mistaken analysis of seismic readings (see page 61): "8 and 10 seconds respectively, top to bottom." At www.911review.org, the estimate for each is "about 15 seconds, which is about the time it would take for a free-fall from that height."

The difficulty comes from analyzing news footage from partially obstructed angles, or images shrouded in debris clouds. Additionally, NIST states, "From video evidence, significant portions of the cores of both buildings (roughly 60 stories of WTC 1 and 40 stories of WTC 2) are known to have stood 15 to 25 seconds after collapse initiation before they, too, began to collapse."

At least the starting point is clearer: The North Tower was 1,368 feet tall, and the South Tower 1,362 feet (excluding spires), or about 417 and 415 meters, respectively. Descent times in a vacuum can be determined through the equation

Height = 0.5 x the Gravitational constant (9.8 meters per second squared) x Time squared. In free fall, the tops of both buildings would have hit the ground in roughly 9.2 seconds. Anything less would have required the debris, either through force from above or negative pressure from below, to have been accelerated at a rate faster than gravity. There is no evidence that either of those things happened. "Some early reports . . . stated that the North Tower collapsed in 8 seconds, while the South Tower did so in 10 seconds," Kausel writes in his analysis "Inferno at the World Trade Center." "The former estimate is surely in error, because it takes an object falling freely from a height of 1350 feet—the (approximate) height of the towers—some 9 seconds to reach the ground."

Professors and investigators contend it's not surprising that their collapse-time estimates are close to would-be free-fall results. In "Why Did the World Trade Center Collapse? Science, Engineering, and Speculation," Thomas W. Eagar, the Thomas Lord Professor of Materials Engineering and Engineering Systems at MIT, estimated each tower fell "within ten seconds." His analysis explains that as exterior columns bowed and joists on the most heavily burned floors gave way, the mass of the collapsing floors created a cascade of failures. "The floor below (with its 1,300-ton design capacity) could not support the roughly 45,000 tons of ten floors (or more) above crashing down," he wrote. "This started the domino effect that caused the buildings to collapse within ten seconds, hitting bottom with an estimated speed of 200 kilometers per hour (125 miles per hour)."

In 2007, Keith Seffen, a senior lecturer in the engineering department at the University of Cambridge, published a paper in the February 2008 *Journal of Engineering Mechanics*, which is published by the American Society of Civil Engineers (ASCE). Most of the research into the towers' collapses, he wrote, had logically focused on the causes of the failures; he was curious about the towers' responses *while* they collapsed. Prior studies "rightly show that the combination of fire and impact damage severely impaired those parts of the building close to where the aircraft hit to hold the weight of the building above," said Seffen. "The top parts were bound to fall down but it was not clear why the undamaged building should have offered little resistance to these falling parts."

In his paper, "Progressive Collapse of the World Trade Centre: a Simple Analysis," Seffen calculated the strength of the floors away from the immediate damage, leading to a "residual capacity" value for the buildings, or the structures' ability to resist collapse once hit. From there he was able to demonstrate that the expected collapse times based on the preceding events would be only 10 seconds. Seffen's research led conspiracy theorists like Peter Wakefield Suit, who has written about a cruise missile hitting the Pentagon at his site www.odeion.org, to label him "an accessory after the fact in the crime of mass-murder."

NIST's final report on the collapse of the Twin Towers offers a simple analysis for why the speeds were so great: "Since the stories below the level of collapse initiation provided little resistance to the tremendous energy released by the falling building mass, the building section above came down essentially in free fall, as seen in videos. As the stories below sequentially failed, the falling mass increased, further increasing the demand on the floors below, which were unable to arrest the moving mass." In a follow-up FAQ that responded to popular conspiracy theories, the agency elaborated: "The elapsed times for the first exterior panels to strike the ground after the collapse initiated in each of the towers (were) approximately 11 seconds for WTC 1 and approximately 9 seconds for WTC 2." It added, "Neither the duration of the seismic records nor video evidence (due to obstruction of view caused by debris clouds) are reliable indicators of the total time it took for each building to collapse completely."

## Puffs of Dust

CLAIM: As each tower collapsed, clearly visible puffs of dust and debris were ejected from the sides of the buildings. In an advertisement in the *New York Times* for the book *Painful Questions: An Analysis of the September 11th Attack,* by software engineer Eric Hufschmid, this assertion was made: "The concrete clouds shooting out of the buildings are not possible from a mere collapse. They do occur from explosions."

In the months following the attacks, numerous conspiracy theorists in addition to Hufschmid cited the comments by Van Romero, an explosives expert and vice president of the New Mexico Institute of Mining and Technology. On September 11, the *Albuquerque Journal* quoted Romero as saying, "My opinion is, based on the videotapes, there were some explosive devices inside the buildings that caused the towers to collapse." The article continued: "Romero said the collapse of the structures resembled those of controlled implosions used to demolish old structures."

Another widely cited argument for the idea that the Twin Towers were brought down by explosives came in November 2005 from BYU's Jones, who argued that, among other things, the manner in which the buildings fell defied the laws of physics. His hypothesis: "The core columns on lower floors are cut using explosives/incendiaries, near-simultaneously, along with cutting charges detonated up higher so that gravity acting on now-unsupported floors helps bring down the buildings quickly." He notes elsewhere, "None of the government-funded studies have provided serious analyses of the explosive demolition hypothesis at all. Until the above steps are taken, the case for accusing ill-trained Muslims of causing all the destruction on 9-11-01 is far from compelling. It just does not add up."

**FACT:** In the decade since September 11, 2001, there have been no fewer than 50 scientific, peer-reviewed journal articles and international symposia presentations about the collapse of the Twin Towers. The findings of professors, engineers, federal employees, and private contractors, which appear in publications as varied as the *Journal of Failure Analysis and Prevention, Practice Periodical on Structural Design and Construction,* and *Welding Journal,* all agree: The towers fell as a result of fires that weakened steel beams and columns near the points of the plane impacts.

The fires themselves likely would not have brought down the towers, but in combination with the damage from the crashes they proved fatal. Once the perimeter columns began to bow inward, the weight of all the floors above the collapsed zone bore down with pulverizing force on the highest intact floor. Unable to absorb the massive energy, that floor failed, transmitting the forces to the floor below, allowing the collapse to progress downward through the building in a chain reaction. Engineers call the process *pancaking,* and it does not require an explosion to begin, according to David Biggs, a structural engineer at Troy, New York–based Ryan-Biggs Associates and a member of the ASCE team that worked on FEMA's *World Trade Center Building Performance Study.*

Like the vast majority of office buildings, the Twin Towers were mostly air. As the floors collapsed onto the ones below, all that air—along with the concrete, drywall, and other debris pulverized by the force of the collapse—was ejected with enormous energy. "When you have a significant portion of a floor collapsing, it's going to shoot air and concrete dust out the window," NIST lead investigator Shyam Sunder first told *Popular Mechanics* five years ago. Those clouds of dust may create the impression of a controlled demolition to untrained eyes, Sunder added, "but it is the floor pancaking that leads to that perception."

The word choice provided a prime opportunity for conspiracists to spin misinformation. "There is strong evidence for controlled demolition causing the collapses instead of fires from the planes . . . but virtually none for the pancake theory of collapse," wrote Crockett Grabbe, a former research scientist in the University of Iowa's

Department of Physics and Astronomy, at www.sealane.org. But conspiracists like Grabbe misstate a crucial point: NIST's investigation focused on the causes of the collapses. "The focus of the investigation was on the sequence of events from the instant of aircraft impact to the initiation of collapse for each tower," NIST wrote in the report's Executive Summary. Sunder never suggested the Twin Towers began to collapse due to pancaking.

The agency further clarified its position in a 2006 online FAQ: "NIST's findings do not support the 'pancake theory' of collapse (initiation), which is premised on a progressive failure of the floor systems in the WTC towers. . . . Instead, the NIST investigation showed conclusively that the failure of the inwardly bowed perimeter columns initiated collapse and that the occurrence of this inward bowing required the sagging floors to remain connected to the columns and pull the columns inwards." Conspiracy theorists promptly leveled accusations that the agency had backtracked. "It is gratifying that NIST finally admits their findings do not support the 'Pancake Theory' of collapse," wrote Kevin Ryan at www. stj911.org. "Note that this is in direct contradiction to Shyam Sunder's comments reported by *Popular Mechanics Magazine*."

Ryan, too, did not read NIST's work carefully. "Of the 28 floor truss connectors at or below the impact floors for WTC 1 [studied by investigators], 93 percent were either missing or bent downward," according to NIST's supporting report NCSTAR 1-3. "Similar results were found for WTC 2, where 88 percent of the floor truss connectors below the impact floors were bent down or missing. . . . This occurrence was most likely a result of the overloading of the lower floors ('pancaking' mechanism) during collapse of the building." The phenomenon most likely occurred, according to NIST— it simply wasn't the initiating event.

This being the case, structural engineer Jon Magnusson says the subsequent air ejections are no surprise. "That happens because the air is going to find wherever the weakest points are," he says. "You could actually have a collapse starting at the top of the building, and the air could come out of the bottom, going down the elevator shafts. It finds the path of least resistance."

Four executives with world-renowned demolition and structural engineering firms, who did not participate in the FEMA or NIST studies, told *Popular Mechanics* the discharges of dust did not indicate the presence of explosives. One of those executives was Mark Loizeaux of Controlled Demolition, Inc., a Phoenix, Maryland, company founded by his father in 1947. Loizeaux's company, which is still family-owned, holds the world records for the largest building by volume ever demolished with explosives (the Seattle Kingdome in 2000) and the tallest building ever imploded (the 439-foot tall J. L. Hudson department store in Detroit in 1998). In an interview with *Popular Mechanics*, Loizeaux said the conspiracy theorists are "absolutely incorrect" in their interpretation of the dust.

"If you look at any building that is imploded, the explosives are primarily placed on the ground floor and the basement," Loizeaux stated. "Why? Because you want to remove the columns when you have the majority of that stored potential energy above where you're taking the columns out. You want to release as much energy as possible. If you look at the collapse of these structures, they start collapsing up where the planes hit. They don't start collapsing down below." Loizeaux said even if explosives had been placed on the upper floors, they would have generated significantly more dust and debris than mere "puffs."

Despite his credentials as a BYU physicist, Jones is among those who have made faulty assumptions about controlled demolition. In putting forth his case that the buildings were brought down with explosives, Jones wrote: "Roughly 2,000 pounds of RDX grade linear-shaped charges (which could have been pre-positioned by just a few men) would then suffice in each Tower and WTC 7 to cut the supports at key points so that gravity would bring the buildings straight down."

According to Loizeaux, Jones is simply wrong. "The explosives configuration manufacturing technology [to bring down those buildings] does not exist," Loizeaux said. "If someone were to attempt to make such charges, they would weigh thousands of pounds apiece. You would need forklifts to bring them into the building."

The biggest commercially available charges, Loizeaux told *Popular Mechanics*, are able to cut through steel that is three inches thick. The box columns at the base of the World Trade Center towers were 14 inches on a side. If big enough charges did exist, Loizeaux said, for each tower it could hypothetically take as long as two months for a team of up to 75 men with unfettered access to three floors to strip the fireproofing off the columns and then place and wire the charges.

"There's just no way to do it," said Loizeaux, adding that it is similarly implausible that explosives could be smuggled into the buildings. "If you just put bulk explosives in file cabinets next to every column in the building, it wouldn't knock those columns down. It would blow the windows out. It would trash the [building] and probably blow out two floors above and a floor below . . . but it wouldn't knock the [building] down."

It should be noted that Jones's primary field of study at BYU was metal catalyzed, or cold, fusion, a specialty that is unrelated to engineering or the performance of tall buildings. Yet he challenged the conclusions of some of the world's leading engineering experts, such as Northwestern University's Zdenek Bazant. One of only 18 people ever to be awarded the Prager Medal for outstanding contributions to either theoretical or experimental solid mechanics, Bazant wrote a paper, published in the *Journal of Engineering Mechanics* in January 2002, outlining his theory of the towers' collapse. Though at that early date Bazant did not have access to all the data, his conclusions were similar to those reached later by NIST researchers.

Jones, however, contended he found a fatal flaw in Bazant's report: The engineer assumed that the steel columns were exposed to temperatures exceeding 800 degrees Celsius (1,472 degrees Fahrenheit). Asked to respond, Bazant emailed *Popular Mechanics*:

> "Today it is clear that the temperatures were much lower, but this is unimportant for my analysis. Structural steel begins to creep already at less than 400 degrees C [about 750 degrees Fahrenheit], and that is enough to cause viscoplastic (creep) buckling.

Also, I was not sure whether the framed tube columns buckled over the height of many floors or one floor. Today we know from accurate photo analysis and from the NIST study that the initial buckling actually occurred over the height of several floors, with the initial imperfection (i.e., lateral inward displacement) caused by the horizontal pull of floor trusses. Multifloor buckling provides less resistance to collapse than single-floor buckling. Anyway, my analysis (and the figures) assumed both possibilities, and in either case the energy dissipation was shown insufficient to arrest the collapse."

Bazant added that he considered it fruitless to engage Jones in a debate. "It would be like trying to prove Einstein's theory to someone who has not taken the relevant graduate courses," Bazant wrote. Indeed, BYU's own engineering department distanced itself from Jones's findings, saying it was "not convinced that his analyses and hypotheses have been submitted to relevant scientific venues that would ensure rigorous technical peer review."

Like many engineering and other experts, Bazant is leery about being drawn into debates with conspiracy theory believers. Some who have spoken up have become targets of accusations and invective, including Romero of the New Mexico Institute of Mining and Technology, who is prominently referenced by many Internet investigators. "I was misquoted in saying that I thought it was explosives that brought down the building," Romero told *Popular Mechanics*. "I only said that that's what it looked like."

Romero said he agrees with the widely accepted scientific explanation for the collapses and wanted to set the record straight. The *Albuquerque Journal* printed a follow-up story on September 22, 2001. "I felt like my scientific reputation was on the line," he stated.

But that explanation of events did not convince some conspiracy theorists, including the Web site www.emperors-clothes.com, which questioned Romero's motives: "The paymaster of Romero's research institute is the Pentagon. Directly or indirectly, pressure was brought to bear, forcing Romero to retract his original statement." Romero found that accusation equally ridiculous: "Conspiracy theorists came out saying that the government got to me. That is the furthest thing from the truth."

Mark Loizeaux has also been the target of accusations. Because of his company's prominence in the demolition field, many conspiracy theorists see it as the likely perpetrator if, as they believe, the towers were brought down by explosives. Loizeaux says that he and other family members have received death threats as well as dozens of e-mails that accuse them of being murderers. "It is hurtful not only to us," he says, "it is hurtful to the people who lost loved ones. It is hurtful to logical, sensitive, injured Americans. And we were all injured on that day."

# "Nano-Thermite" in the Towers

**CLAIM:** With Jones's 2005 theories about RDX charges in Towers 1 and 2 thoroughly debunked, conspiracies about controlled demolition were forced to evolve. The most recent theory appeared in the *Open Chemical Physics Journal* in April 2009, in a paper titled, "Active Thermitic Material Discovered in Dust from the 9/11 World Trade Center Catastrophe." In it, Jones, along with eight others, asserts that four dust samples collected near Ground Zero show chemical traces of unreacted thermite, an aluminum powder and metal oxide mixture that burns at up to 4,500 degrees Fahrenheit (2,482 Celsius) when ignited. (Lava's peak temperature is roughly 2,200 degrees Fahrenheit [1,204 Celsius].) Thermite doesn't explode when it reacts; its high burn temperatures on a localized area make it a tool for cutting through metal. In military applications, for instance, it is used to destroy weapons caches.

The paper states that the group found multicolored "chips" containing both iron oxide and aluminum in the dust. Further, the group speculates that because the identified iron oxide grains are so small—approximately 100 nanometers across—the demolition of the World Trade Center towers was brought about with ultra-fine-grain "nano-thermite," or "super-thermite." The paper concludes: "The red layer of the red/gray chips we have discovered in the WTC dust is active, unreacted thermitic material, incorporating nanotechnology, and is a highly energetic pyrotechnic or explosive material."

With that material, conspiracy theorists say, "those committing the crimes" could have rigged key columns to destroy the towers. "The buildings were brought down so as to make it look like the impact of the planes and the resulting fires might have caused their unprecedented, symmetrical destruction," Kevin Ryan writes at www.journalof911studies.

com. "Those committing the crimes needed to create fire where it would not have existed otherwise, and draw attention toward the part of the buildings where the planes impacted (or in the case of WTC 7, away from the building altogether). This was most probably accomplished through the use of nano-thermites." For added evidence, conspiracy theorists point to images of molten metal spilling from the northeast corner of the South Tower's 80th floor.

**FACT:** This theory suffers multiple failures, beginning with the tangible photographic "evidence" conspiracists cite. As discussed on page 38, the temperatures in the towers reached 1,000 degrees Celsius (1,832 Fahrenheit), far shy of the 1,510 degrees Celsius (2,750 Fahrenheit) required to melt steel. Aluminum, however, can melt at as little as 475 degrees Celsius (887 Fahrenheit).

According to the National Aluminum Association, "The airframe of a typical modern commercial transport aircraft is 80 percent aluminum by weight." A few composite fuselages have made headlines today in aircraft like the Boeing 787, but Boeing 767s began production in 1978. The 767 that carried Flight 175, registered N612UA, was built in 1983. That airliner had an operating empty weight—the weight of the plane's structure, power plant, and furnishings, excluding passengers and fuel—of slightly more than 180,000 pounds. At 9:02 a.m. on September 11, more than 140,000 pounds of aluminum slammed into the south face of WTC 2. According to NIST, "The damage (to the tower) was most severe on the 80th and 81st floors, hit directly by the fuselage."

The fires that would destroy the building began to rage, according to NIST, "especially on the northeast end of the 81 and 82 floors, where the aircraft had bulldozed the office desks and chairs and added its own combustibles." Floors began sagging. Nearly 50 minutes later, molten metal flowed from window 80-255 on the north side of WTC 2. Over the next 7 minutes, before the tower collapsed, the metal flow migrated from that window to neighboring 80-256 on the east, suggesting the molten stream was finding a lower point as the floors shifted. Thermite connected to a column wouldn't have that capability. According to the institute, "NIST concluded that the source of the molten material was aluminum alloys from the aircraft, since these are known to melt between 475 degrees Celsius and 640 degrees Celsius (depending on the particular alloy), well below the expected temperatures (about 1,000 degrees Celsius), in the vicinity of the fires." (In Fahrenheit, the melting range is between 887 degrees and 1,184 degrees, while expected temperatures were in the range of 1,832 degrees.)

Richard Fruehan, professor of metallurgical engineering at Carnegie Mellon University, says Jones has not provided adequate evidence to show that thermite reactions did take place. However, even if they did, that would not necessarily indicate the presence of explosives. "The thermite reaction could have occurred with aluminum metal and any oxide that happens to be near it. Or oxygen could react with aluminum as well. There was a lot of aluminum in the building itself—the windows, etc., plus the airplane's aluminum. That could have caused a thermite reaction and produced a small amount of molten iron." Alan Pense, professor emeritus of metallurgical engineering at Lehigh University, is more direct: "I don't know of anyone else who thinks thermite reactions on steel columns could have done that," he says.

In addition, NIST estimated that it would take .13 pounds of thermite to heat a pound of a steel section to the necessary weakening point—which would require literally tons of thermite to cause the extensive column damage that Flight 175 wrought in WTC 2. That again brings up the challenges of wiring the tower clandestinely. As NIST described it, "Many thousands of pounds of thermite would need to have been placed inconspicuously ahead of time, remotely ignited, and somehow held in direct contact with the surface of hundreds of massive structural components to weaken the building. This makes it an unlikely substance for achieving a controlled demolition."

Finally, because headlines at sites like www.911truth.org attempt to lend credibility to the study by declaring it, "Another Peer Reviewed Paper Published in (a) Scientific Journal," it bears examining what sort of peer review process the paper received, and how scientific the journal it appeared in really is.

The *Open Chemical Physics Journal* is one of "over 250 peer-reviewed open access journals" published by Bentham Science, according to the company's Web site. The business model inverts the pricey subscription fees for scientific journals, making the publications free to readers while charging the authors a few hundred dollars to publish their work. Chemist Niels Harrit, one of Jones's coauthors on the paper, claimed on www.videnskab.dk, a Danish science and research news site, to know the two researchers who reviewed the paper, but he refused to release their names. Meanwhile, at least two U.S. researchers have found Bentham's peer review process highly suspect.

In January 2009, after receiving numerous spam e-mails from Bentham soliciting articles, Philip Davis, a PhD student at Cornell University, and Kent Anderson, of the New England Journal of Medicine, tested the process at the Bentham's *Open Information Science Journal.* They submitted a nonsensical, computer-generated paper titled "Deconstructing Access Points," and listed the Center for Research in Applied Phrenology (CRAP) as their home institution. Four months later, the journal accepted the article after supposed peer review, according to Davis's correspondence with Bentham, which then asked him to send $800 to the Sharjah Airport International Free Zone, a tax-free haven in the United Arab Emirates, for its publication. (At that point, Davis retracted the paper, saying, "We have discovered several errors in the manuscript which question both the validity of the study and the results"—and never heard from Bentham again.) "We cannot conclude that Bentham Science journals practice no peer review," Davis wrote at scholarlykitchen.sspnet.org, "only that it is inconsistently applied."

More inconsistencies surround the publication of Jones's paper on nano-thermite—specifically concerning lines of communication at the journal in which it appeared. The editor-in-chief of the *Open Chemical Physics Journal*, Marie-Paule Pileni, Director of the Mesoscopic and Nanometric Materials Laboratory at France's Université Pierre et Marie Curie, wasn't even aware of the appearance of Jones's work until reached by reporters at www.videnskab.dk. She immediately resigned her position at the chemical physics publication. "They have printed the article without my permission," she explained to the news site, according to a translation. "I cannot accept that this topic is published in my journal. The article has nothing to do with physical chemistry or chemical physics, and I could well believe that there is a political viewpoint behind its publication. If anyone had asked me, I would say that the article should never have been published in this journal. Period."

# Seismic Spikes

**CLAIM:** Seismographs at Columbia University's Lamont-Doherty observatory in Palisades, New York, 21 miles north of the World Trade Center, recorded two enormous spikes, conspiracists claim, showing that explosions actually brought down the Twin Towers. "The strongest jolts were all registered at the beginning of the collapses, well before the falling debris struck the earth," reports the Web site www.whatreallyhappened.com.

Randy Lavello, a columnist on www.prisonplanet.com, a Web site run by radio talk-show host Alex Jones, maintains the seismic spikes are "indisputable proof that massive explosions brought down those towers." Each "sharp spike of short duration," Lavello adds, is consistent with "demolition-style implosions."

**FACT:** The Columbia seismologists who issued the report in question say the conspiracy theorists misinterpret their data and draw erroneous conclusions.

"There is no scientific basis for the conclusion that explosions brought down the towers," Arthur Lerner-Lam, one of the authors of the report, tells *Popular Mechanics*. One of Lerner-Lam's coauthors, Won-Young Kim, adds, "I never spoke with Lavello, and the representation of our work is categorically incorrect and not in context." Concludes Lerner-Lam: "Nothing in the signal suggests this is anything more than an ordinary building collapse. And there's nothing in the signal that suggests an explosion."

The report, titled *Seismic Waves Generated by Aircraft Impacts and Building Collapses at World Trade Center, New York City*, was released in November 2001. It shows graphs that chart the seismic signals produced by both plane crashes, as well as both building collapses.

The impact of the planes barely registered on the Richter scale (neither hit 1.0) despite the massive kinetic energy associated with the impact and combustion of more than 33 tons of jet fuel. This is consistent with similar scenarios, as large explosions typically do not generate the ground motion that seismic readings measure. The 1993 truck bomb at the World Trade Center, in which approximately a half ton of explosives was detonated in the parking garage of the North Tower, was not detected seismically by a monitoring station less than 10 miles away.

The towers' collapses reached a peak Richter scale reading of 2.3. "A Richter reading of 2.3 is pretty small," explains Eric Terrill, Ph.D., director of the Coastal Observing Research and Development Center at the University of California, San Diego. "A 2.3 is generally not felt by humans, but definitely recorded by the seismic sensors." By comparison, an earthquake generally doesn't do much structural damage to buildings until it reaches 4.0. Because the Richter scale is a logarithmic scale, a reading of 4.0 represents a signal nearly 100 times more powerful than that of 2.3 reading.

In both collapses, the readings show small waves that grow progressively higher as the buildings rumble to the ground. The South Tower collapsed in a span of about 10 seconds, while the North Tower fell in about 12 seconds.

How did the conspiracy sites misread the charts? On www.whatreallyhappened.com, the Web site references a graph showing the readings over a 30-minute span. Measured over such a long time period, the collapses do appear as sudden, momentary spikes. But when shown on a more detailed graph covering a 40-second span, it is clear there was sustained seismic activity for the duration of the collapses. (See graphs 12 and 13 in the photo section.)

"Some people misinterpreted the seismic signals," Won-Young Kim says. "There are no huge spikes at the beginning of each tower's respective collapse."

In any case, Web sites like www.prisonplanet.com are wrong to assume that sharp spikes indicate a demolition. A controlled demolition consists of numerous relatively small explosions, not one massive explosion. For example, in Oklahoma City, the truck bomb detonated by Timothy McVeigh outside the Alfred P. Murrah Federal Building released about 28 times as much energy as the explosives used in the later demolition of the building, according to a 1996 article in *American Geophysical Union.* Yet on the day of the bombing, the seismograph operator originally ignored the minor disturbance on the chart, attributing it to local traffic.

"Demolitions are typically very small explosions," Lerner-Lam says. "And you wouldn't record them anyway because they'd typically be aboveground, and too small to observe."

# 3

# WORLD TRADE CENTER BUILDING 7

Ten years after the attacks, many "independent researchers" claim World Trade Center Building 7 remains the "smoking gun" from September 11. The 47-floor highrise took up a full city block just north of the main WTC complex; the tower, completed in 1987, contained nearly two million square feet of floor space, or roughly three-quarters of that in the 102-story Empire State Building. Some of those floors housed high-profile tenants: the offices of the Secret Service (SS), Central Intelligence Agency (CIA), Department of Defense (DOD), Internal Revenue Service (IRS), theSecurities and Exchange Commission (SEC), and the city's Office of Emergency Management (OEM). No plane struck the building on 9/11; at 5:20 p.m., seven and a half hours after the collapse of the South Tower (WTC 2), and seven hours after the collapse of the North Tower (WTC 1), Building 7 plunged to the ground.

FEMA released a building performance study eight months later that focused on long-burning fires as the cause of collapse. WTC 7, investigators pointed out, housed five storage tanks containing some 42,000 gallons of diesel fuel that could power 14 backup generators located throughout the building. That fuel, they speculated, might have fed the flames long enough for them to weaken the building's steel structure. The report noted, however, "The specifics of the fires in WTC 7 and how they caused the building to collapse remain unknown at this time. Although the total diesel fuel on the premises contained massive potential energy, the best hypothesis has only a low probability of occurrence."

In June 2004, NIST released a progress report that modified those findings, and hypothesized that WTC 7 was far more compromised by debris from the destruction of Tower 1, about 300 feet away, than FEMA's report indicated. NIST discovered previously undocumented damage to WTC 7's upper stories and its southwest corner, writing at the time, "the south face of WTC 7 was obscured by smoke, making direct observation of damage from photographs or videos difficult or impossible. . . . Large fires were burning in WTC 5 and WTC 6, as well as those noted in WTC 7." In other words, in the many photographs taken of the area following the attacks—a primary source in the FEMA report—the structure of WTC 7 is simply not visible. One of the few clear photographs, which was taken by the New York City Police Department, reveals that the exterior damage from debris to the building was indeed severe.

After that update, NIST's investigative team was assigned full-time to completing the analysis of the Twin Towers' collapse. Once the 10,000-page final report on WTC 1 and 2 was released at the end of October 2005, investigators spent three years testing hypotheses about the collapse of Building 7. When the final report was released in November 2008, conspiracy theorists had had ample opportunity for speculation.

As investigators grappled with a collapse that made architectural history, conspiracists struggled just as mightily to concoct a valid motivation for the government to have destroyed the building. "Researchers have been forced to speculate about the motives for including WTC 7 in the 9/11 destruction," writes Ronald Bleier at the Demographic, Environmental, and Security Issues Project Web site (desip. igc.org). "I join many in the 9/11 inquiry movement who find it plausible that [the OEM] housed the command center for the destruction of the Twin Towers as well as a homing device bringing the planes to their targets. Many think that the building was brought down to destroy the equipment and the computers involved in the conspiracy." Other theories center on leaseholder Larry Silverstein trying to collect insurance money or shadowy figures plotting to destroy case files at the SEC.

Whatever the storyline, however, conspiracy theorists almost universally agree on one thing: The building, they say, was brought down with pre-planted explosives through a controlled demolition. "In the case of WTC 7 . . . there could be no doubt that all the columns, or most of the columns, must have been severed simultaneously," writes Frank Legge, one of the independent researchers at Scholars for 9/11 Truth & Justice. The reality, according to investigators, is simultaneously less complicated and even more remarkable.

# Fire and Debris Damage

**CLAIM:** Seven hours after the second Twin Tower fell, WTC 7 collapsed. The 47-story building housed offices for the Secret Service and CIA, among others—and was therefore, conspiracists say, a repository of secrets and evidence that needed to be destroyed. "Many researchers believe that shadowy elements within the agencies housed in WTC 7 are prime suspects in this sprawling conspiracy. . . . If they are correct, Building 7 was literally a nest of suspicious activity and its remaining intact may well have been a catastrophe for those who were counting on its destruction," wrote Jeremy Baker on the Web site www. serendipity.li.

How did these "shadowy elements" engineer the collapse? As with the Twin Towers, conspiracy theorists see evidence of a controlled demolition. According to the Web site www. jesus-is-savior.com, "No combination of debris damage, fuel-tank explosions, and fires could inflict the kind of simultaneous damage to all the building's columns required to make the building implode."

**FACT:** The collapse of WTC 7 was initially puzzling to investigators, but they are now convinced the building failed primarily as a result of the long-burning fires in its interior. This conclusion is a modification of NIST's initial hypothesis, released as part of its June 2004 *Progress Report on the Federal Building and Fire Safety Investigation of the World Trade Center Disaster*, which attributed the collapse at least partly to destruction on the south side of the tower. "The most important thing we found was that there was, in fact, physical damage to the south face of building 7," NIST's Shyam Sunder told *Popular Mechanics* at the time. "On about a third of the face to the center and to the bottom—approximately 10 stories—about 25 percent of the depth of the building was scooped out." A three-year investigation by the agency has now shown, however, that the tower's collapse was initiated by the expansion of steel beams in the fires—and that WTC 7 would have probably collapsed regardless of the debris damage.

That said, the fatal fires wouldn't have started without the debris damage. A seismology report prepared at Columbia University notes that the collapses of the Twin Towers caused little ground instability, but nevertheless discharged a massive amount of energy—as much as 107 joules in the kinetic energy of dust and debris. Except for temperature, the effect was similar to the energy contained in the pyroclastic ash given off in volcanic eruptions. "Only a very small portion of the [gravitational energy associated with the collapse of each tower] was converted into seismic waves," the report states. "Most of the energy went into the deformation of buildings and the formation of rubble and dust." The fires that doomed Building 7 began with burning debris from the North Tower at about 10:28 a.m.

They started small, single cubicle fires on at least ten separate floors on the south and southwest of the building. Adjacent cubicles caught fire—followed by cubicle clusters across aisles, ignited by thermal radiation from the flames. Offices were superheated until various surfaces reached their autoignition temperatures and burst into flames, a process known as *flashover*. The radiated heat spread fire to adjacent offices and down the halls. Unlike in Towers 1 and 2, the majority of the building's fireproofing was still intact when the burn began. The primary and backup water supplies for the building's sprinkler systems, however, were effectively eliminated by the collapse of the Twin Towers, which damaged water lines. On floors 7 through 9 and 11 through 13 in WTC 7, the fires began burning out of control.

Most of the floors in WTC 7 had combustible fuel loads—cubicle walls, desks, bookshelves, and paperwork—of roughly 4 pounds per square foot, equivalent to what was found in WTC 1 and 2. On floors 11 and 12, which were occupied by the SEC, NIST's investigative team estimated fuel loads 50 percent higher due to a higher density of paper materials. That was critical: in WTC 7 there was no jet fuel to incite a blaze, the way there was in the Twin Towers. Instead, the fires grew from one workstation to another, until by 4:00 p.m. they had concentrated on the northeast corner of the building. This was important to the collapse: The top 40 floors of WTC 7 were supported by 24 interior columns and 58 perimeter columns. Twenty-one of those interior columns formed a rectangular building core; the remaining three interior columns—numbered 79, 80, and 81—were offset to the east, and were larger in diameter because they supported long floor spans on that side of the building.

The fires in WTC 7 generally burned at lower temperatures than in the North and South Towers. Some pockets reached 593 degrees Celsius (1,100 Fahrenheit), comparable to WTC 1 and 2, but the fires mostly peaked around 299 degrees Celsius (570 Fahrenheit). They weakened the steel beams and columns somewhat, but had another, more profound impact: The heat caused 30-foot steel beams that supported the floors in the northeast corner to expand—0.0000065 inches per inch of original length for each degree Fahrenheit, a process known as "thermal expansion." "Anyone who has run a tight jar lid under water to help loosen it knows that the metal expands when it gets hot," Sunder says. "Heat also causes steel to lose strength and stiffness. But thermal expansion occurs at temperatures much lower than those required to reduce steel strength and stiffness." At that coefficient of expansion, a 50-foot steel beam increases in length by .39 inches—more than one-third of an inch—for every increase of 100 degrees Fahrenheit. Based on the temperatures inside WTC 7, key floor beams increased in length by more than 4.25 inches in the northeast section of the building.

At floor 13, that expansion sheared the bolts that connected Column 79, in the northeast corner of the building's interior, to the girder reaching across to Column 44 on the tower's north face. At approximately 5:20 p.m., continued expansion pushed the girder entirely off the seat holding it against Column 79, sending floor 13 collapsing onto the floors below. A cascade of floor failures followed, according to NIST, leaving Column 79—which supported approximately 2,000 square feet of floor space—with insufficient lateral support between floors 5 and 14. The weight of the 33 floors above buckled Column 79 eastward, beginning a progressive collapse of the upper floors on the northeast corner. The sudden load redistribution, coupled with debris damage from the falling floors, buckled nearby Columns 80 and 81, according to NIST, initiating an east-to-west chain reaction of interior column failures. With the core in ruins, load redistribution from the gutted building buckled the exterior columns between floors 7 and 14 and brought down the exterior of the tower.

NIST's final analysis, of course, differs from what the agency first suggested to *Popular Mechanics* in 2004. Two years earlier, FEMA first hypothesized in its *World Trade Center Building Performance Study* that WTC 7 collapsed almost exclusively due to the fires; the conspiracy movement seized on this assertion, noting that there were no other examples of large fire-protected steel buildings collapsing because of fire alone. When NIST's final report agreed that, "This was the first known instance of the total collapse of a tall building primarily due to fires," conspiracists pounced again. At www.globalresearch.ca, David Ray Griffin wrote, "If NIST did engage in fraudulent science, this would not be particularly surprising. NIST is an agency of the U.S. Department of Commerce. During the years it was writing its World Trade Center reports, therefore, it was an agency of the Bush-Cheney administration."

Sunder prefers to focus on the evidence gathered by an investigative team that included 13 NIST investigators, 59 technical staffers, 15 special experts and consultants, contractors from the private sector, and a 10-person advisory committee of college professors, independent architects, and directors of energy and hazards research centers who provided technical advice. "The public should really recognize the science is really behind what we have said," Sunder concluded. "The obvious stares you in the face."

# Wreckage Pile

**CLAIM:** The tidy pile of wreckage in the footprint of WTC 7 has provided fodder for conspiracy theorists. "Aren't the odds just simply too astronomical that if the fire could weaken the support structures of the WTC 7 enough to fail, that it happened to cause the building to collapse inwards and fall straight down on its own footprint just like a controlled implosion is designed to do?" questions killtown.911review.org.

Other claims distort legitimate information to come to the same conclusion. At the website www.howstuffworks. com, contributing writer Tom Harris put together a primer on controlled demolition with the help of industry expert Brent Blanchard, the operations manager for Protec Documentation Services, which performs vibration consulting and photographic documentation for contractors throughout the world. As an easy visual, they compared one type of demolition to a tree falling in the woods. "The main challenge in bringing a building down is controlling which way it falls," Harris wrote. "Tipping a building over is something like felling a tree. To topple the building to the north, the blasters detonate explosives on the north side of the building first, in the same way you would chop into a tree from the north side if you wanted it to fall in that direction."

The article, published in June 2001, further notes: "Sometimes, though, a building is surrounded by structures that must be preserved. In this case, the blasters proceed with a true implosion, demolishing the building so that it collapses straight down into its own footprint (the total area at the base of the building). This feat requires such skill that only a handful of demolition companies in the world will attempt it."

The analysis provided unintended fodder for conspiracy theorists. In his paper "Why Indeed Did the WTC Buildings Collapse?" Stephen Jones quotes the passage, then writes, "Why would terrorists undertake straight-down collapses of WTC 7 and the Towers, when 'toppling-over' falls would require much less work and would do much more damage in downtown Manhattan? And where would they obtain the necessary skills and access to the buildings for a symmetrical implosion anyway?" He concludes Building 7's collapse into its footprint provides "strong evidence for an 'inside job.'"

**FACT:** According to NIST's exhaustive computer simulations, by the time the exterior of the building collapsed—the dramatic event memorialized in dozens of online videos—much of the collapse had already taken place, out of the view of TV cameras. Inside the building, the eastward buckling of Column 79 began a progressive collapse of the upper floors—leading to the visible kink in the roofline as the east penthouse descended into the building. The sudden load redistribution, coupled with debris damage from the falling floors, buckled nearby Columns 80 and 81. "All the floor connections to these three columns, as well as to the exterior columns, failed, and the floors fell on the east side of the building," states the NIST report. "The exterior façade on the east quarter of the building was just a hollow shell."

The chain reaction of interior column failures led to a buckling of the building's core. When the weight of the collapsing building suddenly shifted to the exterior columns, those supports buckled between floors 7 and 14. The entire building shell above collapsed as a single unit. "What you're seeing is an interior collapse, then (it moves) to the outside," Sunder says. "What you're getting is an impression of a controlled demolition, but it's not."

Meanwhile, Blanchard says that conspiracy theorists have misappropriated his example of felling a tree for multiple reasons. WTC 7 was 330 feet long at its maximum, and 140 feet wide. Unlike tipping a tree a few feet in diameter, tipping WTC 7 would have required deflecting the building more than 70 feet north or south before its center of gravity moved beyond its base—an incomprehensible margin, particularly because WTC 7 sustained no external lateral forces. (WTC 2, which was hit with the faster moving of the two 767s—traveling about 540 miles per hour—swayed 27 *inches* on impact.) The office tower's interconnected frame would help prevent movement that drastic. "When one column or beam is compromised it's going to pull on the rest of the structure, not just shear off," Blanchard says. "Tipping something like Building 7 just can't be done."

Secondly, Blanchard estimates the interior of WTC 7 was some 80 to 90 percent air. (That percentage is lower than the 110-story Towers 1 and 2; Thomas W. Eagar, the Thomas Lord Professor of Materials Engineering and Engineering Systems at MIT, estimates the Twin Towers were each 95 percent air.) Once thousands of tons of steel beams and concrete flooring began to collapse, Blanchard says, the structure had too much inertia to go in any other direction. "Trees are inherently rigid, monolithic structures," Blanchard states. "A radio tower could be felled like a tree. You could begin a building's decent in a certain direction by cutting certain columns, but you cannot fell a building like a tree."

Furthermore, claims of a tidy collapse ignore obvious evidence. The Borough of Manhattan Community College's Fiterman Hall is located across the street from WTC 7, some 150 feet northwest of the tower. The 15-story steel and concrete classroom building sustained such structural damage from the collapse of WTC 7 that it was ultimately scheduled for demolition. The 32-story Verizon building, located due west of Building 7, suffered extensive damage to its east face when its neighbor collapsed. It cost the phone company four years and $322 million to restore the building.

Much like with the collapses of the Twin Towers (see Chapter 2), conspiracy theorists count seconds on grainy news footage and suggest that if the 610-foot-tall WTC 7 collapsed at close to free-fall speed, pre-planted explosives must have removed any interior resistance. At the website www.garlicandgrass.org, which describes itself as "A Grassroots Journal of America's Political Soul," conspiracy theorist Dave Heller writes, "Shortly after 5:20 p.m. on Sept. 11, as the horrific day was coming to a close, WTC7 mysteriously imploded and fell to the ground in an astounding 6.5 seconds. . . . A rock dropped from the 47th floor would have taken at least 6 seconds to hit the ground. WTC7, in its entirety, fell to the earth in 6.5 seconds." He finishes: "Judge for yourself. Watch WTC7 go down. It takes 6.5 seconds. Take out your stopwatch."

NIST, required more precise measurements than those afforded by a stopwatch and an Internet connection. The agency analyzed video footage of the collapse down to the individual pixel on the building's perimeter, noting any shift in brightness that would indicate movement. The moment the east penthouse descended, the clock started; 6.9 seconds later, the exterior began to fall. "The instant of initial movement was estimated by analyzing changes in the color of a pixel in the video recording over time. A single pixel close to the center of the north face roofline was selected and the color of the pixel, expressed as values of hue, saturation, and brightness, was recorded for each frame. . . . The brightness was found to provide the best indicator of change since the brightness of a pixel representing the sky above the building had a value of 100 percent while a pixel representing the roofline of the building (granite façade) had a brightness of roughly 60 percent for the pixel selected."

NIST charted the building's collapse as it fell 18 stories, until the roofline disappeared behind neighboring high-rises. The agency separated the visible collapse into three distinct sections: Stage 1, which lasted 1.75 seconds, corresponds to the initial buckling of the outside columns and the start of the north face's descent. In Stage 2, lasting 2.25 seconds, the building's shell fell 8 stories, or 105 feet, in a "free fall drop." NIST agrees that the exterior fell at gravitational acceleration during this stage, noting that "the columns provided negligible support to the upper portion of the north face." In Stage 3, the upper section of the building encountered resistance from the debris pile below, and it took 1.4 seconds for the northwest corner to fall 130 feet and vanish from view. "The collapse time was approximately 40 percent longer than that of free-fall for the first 18 stories of descent," the report concluded. "The detailed analysis shows that this increase in time is due primarily to Stage 1, in which column buckling was just beginning and gradual increases in displacement and velocity were observed."

NIST also showed that conspiracy theories championing controlled demolition overlook two key gaps in their argument. First, a blast in an office building would be virtually guaranteed to explode windows; conspiracy buffs claim as much when they speculate that window shards ejected from the Twin Towers are proof of explosives (see page 32). Using SHAMRC, a computer program that models explosive detonations, NIST found that affixing 9 pounds of RDX explosives to Column 79—which weighed approximately 1,000 pounds per foot—could have theoretically led to the overall destruction of WTC 7 witnessed on September 11. But even beyond the logical leap that supposes no building tenants witnessed the removal of column enclosures, or workers with welding torches cutting column sections, or the placement of wires for detonation, there's a problem with the theory: SHAMRC simulations showed that nearly every window on the northeast corner of the floor would have been blown out. Photographic evidence from September 11 doesn't show that damage.

Finally, that hypothetical blast event would have had another unmistakable sign: The sound of a massive explosion would have rattled through the corridors of the Financial District. Using NLAWS, a sound wave propagation program developed by the Air Force, NIST found that any blast capable of bringing down WTC 7 would have registered 130 to 140 decibels more than half a mile away from the tower—almost the distance across the Hudson River to New Jersey. "This sound level is consistent with standing next to a jet plane engine and more than 10 times louder than being in front of the speakers at a rock concert," NIST has stated. "Soundtracks from videos being recorded at the time of the collapse did not contain any sound as intense as would have accompanied such a blast. Therefore, the Investigation Team concluded that there was no demolition-type blast that would have been intense enough to lead to the collapse of WTC 7 on September 11, 2001."

# Silverstein's "Pull It" Quote

**CLAIM:** Conspiracy theorists claim that real-estate developer Larry Silverstein, who leased WTC 7 from the Port Authority of New York and New Jersey, admits in a 2002 PBS documentary to intentionally bringing down the building. In this film, *America Rebuilds: A Year at Ground Zero*, Silverstein talks about the WTC 7 collapse: "I remember getting a call from the, er, fire department commander, telling me that they were not sure they were gonna be able to contain the fire, and I said, 'We've had such terrible loss of life, maybe the smartest thing to do is pull it.' And they made that decision to pull and we watched the building collapse."

Later in the documentary, a weary firefighter at Ground Zero notes, "We're getting ready to pull building six." Taken in combination, these comments lead conspiracy theorists to believe that in saying "pull it," Silverstein was authorizing the demolition of WTC 7. An article on the "9/11 Truth Movement" in *New York* magazine put it this way: "Pull it, as Truth people never tire of repeating, is the term usually used for controlled demolition."

**FACT:** Five demolition and engineering experts told *Popular Mechanics* that "pull it" is not slang for controlled demolition. "I've never heard of it," said Jon Magnusson of Magnusson Klemencic Associates. Ron Dokell, retired president of Olshan Demolishing Company, said the same thing.

Mark Loizeaux of Controlled Demolition, Inc. added that the only way he could imagine the term being used is in reference to a process where the legs of a structure are precut and attached to cables, and then large machines are used literally to pull the building to the ground. But he said this is only done with radio towers and relatively small buildings. "There is no way you could pull over structures like the [WTC 7]," Loizeaux wrote in an e-mail to *Popular Mechanics*. "The contractors removing the debris tried on several occasions to pull over sections of [World Trade Center buildings 5 and 6, both less than 10 stories tall] that were damaged by the fire and the collapse."

Brent Blanchard's team from Protec Documentation Services was at Ground Zero in late autumn 2001, photographing the cleanup efforts. He documented WTC 6 being pulled (see one of his photographs on the photo insert). "The building was pulled in a series of three sections," he says. "The frame was pre-cut into pieces so it could fall uniformly. The sections were pulled down by cables attached to the booms of excavators." According to an analysis of the collapse that Blanchard wrote in 2006, "We can say with certainty that a similar operation would have been logistically impossible at Ground Zero on 9/11, physically impossible for a building the size of WTC 7, and the structure did not collapse in that manner anyway."

Silverstein released a statement on September 5, 2005, saying his comments were misinterpreted. He said he was referring to his desire to pull a squadron of firefighters from the building. The statement read in part: "Mr. Silverstein expressed his view that the most important thing was to protect the safety of those firefighters, including, if necessary, to have them withdraw from the building." Firefighters contacted by *Popular Mechanics* confirm that "pull" is a common firefighting term for removing personnel from a dangerous structure.

In addition, NIST is definitive on this count. Shyam Sunder began his August 2008 press conference announcing the agency's findings with this: "Before I tell you what we found, I'd like to tell you what we did not find. We did not find any evidence that explosives were used to bring the building down."

# The Death of Barry Jennings

**CLAIM:** On September 11, Barry Jennings was one of the few people rushing into Building 7. As administrative superintendent for the New York City Housing Authority's Emergency Services Department, he headed to the Office of Emergency Management, housed on the 23rd floor. Jennings and Michael Hess, who led the New York City Law Department as corporation counsel and also reported to the OEM, were the last two people evacuated from the tower.

In 2007, Jennings, the father of four, gave an interview to the producers of *Loose Change*, alleging that he heard "explosions" in Building 7 before it collapsed. "I'm just confused about . . . why World Trade Center 7 went down in the first place," he says on camera. "I know what I heard. I heard explosions." In that instant, Jennings became conspiracy theorists' sole eyewitness for a Building 7 controlled demolition scenario. "Jennings Interview Demolishes Official Version" declared a headline at www.infowars.com.

NIST's analysis of the emergency response at the World Trade Center alludes to Jennings's story, and provides a timeline suggesting the "explosions" he heard were actually the collapse of WTC 1 roughly 300 feet away, along with the subsequent debris damage to Building 7. Jennings backed off his claims during a 2008 interview with the BBC, saying he "didn't like the way (he) was portrayed" in the film. He added, "I didn't appreciate that, so I told them to pull my interview." What is certain, however, is that on August 19, 2008, two days before NIST released its final report on Building 7, Jennings died at the age of 53. Speculation about a government hit began almost immediately.

"In every major cover-up from the JFK assassination to Iran Contra, we can see one common thread. The untimely death of eyewitnesses," wrote radio host Jack Blood at deadlinelive.info. "Barry Jennings was not only an important and most credible eyewitness, but he openly refuted much of the government, and media version of events. He was a liability." Further, the Web site www.jenningsmystery.com issued a "challenge to American Journalism": "No cause of death has been made public, and the mainstream press has not even covered the death of this American hero."

The theory added another layer when Dylan Avery, the director of *Loose Change*, made an April 2009 appearance on Blood's radio show. Avery claimed he had looked into Jennings's death, and discovered "really creepy" things. The Jenningses' former home on Long Island, he said, was now vacant and abandoned. Avery added that he'd even hired a private investigator to look into the cause of death. "A little less than 24 hours later, (we) got a response back [from the P.I.] that said, pretty much word for word, 'Due to some of the information I have uncovered, I have determined this is a job for the police. I have refunded your credit card. Please do not contact me ever again about this individual.'" Blood summarized the situation this way: "If I'm looking at this from an objective point of view, I think something really stinks here. I'd like to think that all of my listeners, and anyone out there who is passionate about what really happened on 9/11, would really want to get to the bottom of this."

**FACT:** Barry Jennings Jr. won't ever forget the day he turned 19. His birthday was spent, he says, at Stony Brook University Hospital on Long Island, watching over his father. Barry Sr. lost his battle with leukemia the next day. "I still hurt every time someone says the government killed him," Jennings Jr. wrote in an online chat room, defending his father's legacy. "It is insulting to me."

According to Jennings Jr., nearly 20 years earlier, Barry Sr.'s twin brother, Larry, died from the same disease. "There's no conspiracy here," says Howard Marder, who worked with Barry Sr. at the Housing Authority. "This disease hit him, and bam, he was suddenly gone. A great guy was taken from us."

Marder, who was a spokesman for the organization before retiring in November 2009, was drawn into the maelstrom when he responded to a request from www.infowars.com reporter Aaron Dykes to verify Jennings's passing. "A spokesperson for the Housing Authority has now confirmed his death, after weeks of rumors circulating online," Dykes wrote, "but refused to give any further details." Marder wonders exactly what they expected. "As soon as he died, conspiracy theorists started calling me from all over the world," he told *Popular Mechanics*. "I really didn't want to give out any information except to say, 'Please, leave his family alone while they grieve.'"

Barry Jr., his brother Jarel, and Barry's widow, Sheba, all declined repeated interview requests from *Popular Mechanics*. But unlike conspiracy theories about stand-down orders or seismic readings, the sometimes-public struggles of the Jennings family over the past two years offer perspective on the human toll of the rumor mongering. Imagine watching a loved one die, then having conspiracy theorists suggest, "Now, let's consider the CIA's capacity to assassinate Barry Jennings and make the cause of death appear to be a heart attack," as did one commenter at 911blogger.com. Or having conspiracists dismiss his entire existence as a sham, as a commenter did at the Reality Shack forums (www.z6.invisionfree.com/Reality_Shack) when he wrote, "Barry Jennings is about as real as James Bond." The result was predictable.

"I guess my father really was a hero, huh?" Jennings Jr. wrote in a biting response at wecanchangetheworld. wordpress.com. "I will admit, watching him die at 53, the day after my birthday, in Stony Brook hospital from leukemia wasn't the highlight of my life. . . . Losing my father at 19 wasn't my plan." Jennings Jr.'s fiancée, Dominique Austin, even entered the fray: "Barry Jennings didn't die because of the government, ok?" she wrote in a forum at www.topix. com. "I've seen everything; you guys didn't see anything. . . . We both stood by his father's side when he was sick and when he died. So talk (about) what you know and not what you don't know." Austin tells *Popular Mechanics* that Jennings Sr.'s death hit her fiancé particularly hard. "Barry Jr. stopped being himself," she says. "For a while, he pushed everyone away. He pushed me away. He doesn't want to talk about it and risk going down that road again." After six years with Barry Jr., she says she, too, feels the loss. "Barry Sr. was a great father," she says. "I looked forward to having him as a father-in-law."

Sadly, things continued downhill for the Jennings family after Barry Sr.'s death. In a biography on his MySpace page, Barry Jr. wrote that about five years ago, Sheba was "stricken with an unknown disease that limited her mobility and strength." The ancillary result of his father's death, the bio says, was his "mother being sent to a nursing home in upstate New York and Barry losing his home." According to public court records, the mortgage holder foreclosed the Jenningses'

Long Island home in August 2009. That's why Avery found the house empty. Sheba lives today in South Carolina.

As evidenced by the declined interviews, the Jennings family seems most interested in putting the past behind them. "It's upsetting for all of us that people keep telling these lies," Austin says. "They don't know the real story." She and Jennings Jr. live together in Long Island, where he's trying to launch a music career—and ignore the conspiracy theorists. "As screwed up as our government may be, at least I can say that they didn't kill my father," he wrote at http://wecanchangetheworld.wordpress.com, "because I watched him die." He concluded with the note, "I'm tired of speaking up. You can believe what you want to."

# Minimal Wreckage to Study

**CLAIM:** The collapses of the buildings left an estimated 1.8 million tons of concrete, steel, and other debris at the World Trade Center site. Much of it was cleared quickly, however, and the minimal amount of wreckage of WTC 7 available for later investigation has generated speculation. Some conspiracists point to the fast removal of debris as evidence of a government cover-up. "The columns were in pieces big enough to ship in a dump truck, which is what happened," writes one truther at www.debate. org. "The WTC wreckage was shipped overseas to china [sic] before any experts could even examine. Would experts not want to analyze the three biggest structural failures in the history of the world?"

**FACT:**   In the eight months following 9/11, workers moved more than 108,000 truckloads of debris to the Fresh Kills Landfill on Staten Island, New York. There, close to a billion individual pieces of debris were sorted by law enforcement officials as part of the largest forensic investigation in U.S. history. "There has been some concern expressed by others that the work of the team has been hampered because debris was removed from the site and has subsequently been processed for recycling," Gene Corley told the U.S. House of Representatives' Committee on Science in March 2002. "This is not the case. The team has had full access to the scrap yards and to the site and has been able to obtain numerous samples. At this point there is no indication that having access to each piece of steel from the World Trade Center would make a significant difference to understanding the performance of the structures."

NIST's investigators examined 236 pieces of steel from the wreckage of Towers 1 and 2, though Shyam Sunder admits that WTC 7 wreckage was more difficult to study. Hundreds of investigators at the salvage yards found that the Twin Towers' steel columns were labeled and numbered, but columns from Buildings 5, 6, and 7 were not. "In general, much less evidence existed for WTC 7 than for the two WTC towers," the agency reported. "The steel for WTC 1 and WTC 2 contained distinguishing characteristics that enabled it to be identified once removed from the site during recovery efforts. However, the same was not true for the WTC 7 steel. Certainly, there is a lot less visual and audio evidence of the WTC 7 collapse compared to the collapses of the WTC 1 and WTC 2 towers, which were much more widely photographed."

NIST relied upon extensive interviews, schematics, studies of the building, and audio and video recordings to analyze fire dynamics and create computer models of WTC 7's collapse. The agency used a program called ANSYS to model events that caused the collapse, and LS-DYNA, which creates fluid 3-D models often used to simulate automobile crashes or the effects of bird strikes in jet engines, to study the behavior of the building's frame during the failure. "Due to the nonlinearities in the analysis, as well as sequential local failures, a 25-second analysis took up to 8 weeks to complete," the report states. NIST added, "Considerable effort was expended to compile evidence and to determine whether intentionally set explosives might have caused the collapse of WTC 7."

Studying steel from Building 7 might have benefited investigators, though Sunder isn't surprised that in the chaotic days following the collapses, labeling scrap metal wasn't the top priority. "At the time, we were concerned about terrorists who attacked our country, and search and rescue operations," he says. "I think the fact that they [investigators] didn't collect [wreckage] was the least important activity that happened that day." In 2002, New York mayor Michael Bloomberg, who graduated from Johns Hopkins University with a degree in electrical engineering, threw his support behind the cleanup efforts, saying, "If you want to take a look at the construction methods and the design, that's in this day and age what computers do. Just looking at a piece of metal generally doesn't tell you anything."

The estimated 200,000 tons of salvaged steel from Ground Zero ultimately found its way to multiple places—

from scrap yards to warships. The Chinese state news service reported that Shanghai Baosteel Group purchased 50,000 tons of scrap WTC steel from a New Jersey company at $120 per ton. The Indian Steel Alliance, an association of major Indian steel producers, estimates that scrap processing companies across the country imported more than 55,000 tons of the WTC steel debris, which was used to create everything from kitchen utensils to college buildings. More recently, the Navy's 684-foot-long USS *New York*, which was commissioned in November 2009, carries 7.5 tons of the recycled steel in its bow stem. Today, there are still about 1,000 objects from the World Trade Center housed in the 80,000-square-foot Hangar 17 at John F. Kennedy International Airport, according to Steven Weintraub, a consultant to the Port Authority on the preservation of 9/11 artifacts. They range from a pair of PATH train cars to 50-ton steel columns. The Port Authority has received about 1,000 requests from municipalities and nonprofit organizations hoping to include the artifacts in local 9/11 memorials.

# 4

# THE PENTAGON

At 9:37 a.m. on September 11, 2001—51 minutes after the first plane hit the World Trade Center—the Pentagon was similarly attacked. The Pentagon is a five-story building in Arlington, Virginia, across the Potomac River from Washington D.C. At the time of the crash, thousands of commuters were crowded in rush-hour traffic along the highways surrounding the headquarters of the Department of Defense. Although hundreds of witnesses saw a Boeing 757 hit the building, some conspiracy advocates insist there is evidence that a missile or a different type of plane smashed into the Pentagon.

French author Thierry Meyssan is arguably the leading promoter of an alternative explanation to the Pentagon destruction. In April 2002, just seven months after the attacks, Meyssan published a book titled *L'Effroyable Imposture* ("The Horrifying Fraud") arguing, in part, that the Pentagon attack was self-inflicted by the U.S. military in order to justify future wars. Meyssan never visited the United States for his research. Though denounced by most French newspapers, Meyssan's book sold more than 200,000 copies in France. Translated into 18 languages, it was published in the United States as *9/11: The Big Lie.* Meyssan's book is not accepted by all conspiracy theorists, but its claims have been widely repeated, notably in the popular documentary *Loose Change.*

One factor that allowed Meyssan to gain converts was the absence of video showing the crash. For almost five years, the only visual evidence of a plane striking the Pentagon was a set of still-frame shots taken from a security camera on the north side of the building. The photos were leaked to several news organizations in 2002. But because the camera was recording at a slow frame rate and the Boeing 757 was traveling at 780 feet per second, the images show little more than a blurry white object approaching the Pentagon and a fireball subsequently erupting from the building.

In 2004, the conservative watchdog group Judicial Watch filed a request under the Freedom of Information Act for the video itself—as opposed to still-frame photos taken from the video. The intention was to disprove Meyssan definitively, says Tom Fitton, president of Judicial Watch.

The Pentagon initially refused the request because the video was among the evidence in the pending trial of accused 9/11 Al Qaeda conspirator Zacarias Moussaoui. In May 2006, after Moussaoui pleaded guilty and was sentenced to life in prison, the Pentagon released two videos showing the crash from slightly different angles. The violence of the footage is undeniable, but to call it video is a stretch: It's actually more like a slide show of the images previously released—a blur followed by a massive explosion. Within hours of the videos being released online, the Web site www.prison planet.com posted a story titled, "New Pentagon Video Shows No Boeing Airliner."

A Pentagon spokesperson tells *Popular Mechanics* that the video was taken with a Philips LTC 1261 security camera and recorded at one frame per second. Jerry Housenga is a technical product specialist with Bosch Security Systems, which bought the Philips camera division in 2002. According to Housenga, it was unrealistic to think that the low-quality security camera footage would reveal the crystal-clear image of a Boeing 757 traveling at 780 feet per second. While most advanced security and surveillance cameras can be set to capture real-time video, the attached recording systems are almost always set at significantly slower frame rates in order to conserve storage space. As a result, it is unlikely that the recording system of any nearby security camera would be set at a rate high enough to capture the speeding plane with decent resolution.

Judicial Watch's Fitton tells *Popular Mechanics* that he was disappointed the footage was not more conclusive. By the same token, the newly released footage also failed to live up to the hopes of conspiracy theorists, who had long argued that the government must have withheld the footage because it contained unequivocal proof that a missile or noncommercial aircraft had hit the building. Fitton's group is pursuing other videos, reportedly seized by the FBI from businesses near the Pentagon, that may show the crash more clearly. But, he adds, "We ought not need a video to understand what happened on that day."

# Flight 77 Debris

**CLAIM:** Conspiracy theorists maintain that the Boeing 757 that struck the Pentagon left suspiciously little wreckage at the point of impact, or on the building's remarkably pristine green lawn. "In reality, a Boeing 757 was never found," claims an animation that appears on www.pentagonstrike.co.uk, a Web site that asks the question, "What hit the Pentagon on 9/11?" The online animation has had wide circulation in the United States and Europe.

Meyssan professes to have the answer. "This kind of weapon does look like a small civilian airplane, but it's not a plane at all," he wrote. Meyssan cites little actual evidence to support his argument, but references an eyewitness who says what hit the Pentagon seemed "like a cruise missile with wings."

**FACT:** Meyssan's contention that someone saw a cruise missile hit the Pentagon is the result of selective editing. The witness, a Washington D.C. broadcaster named Mike Walter, actually told CNN: "I looked out my window and saw this plane, this jet, an American Airlines jet, coming. And I thought, 'This doesn't add up. It's really low.' And I saw it. I mean, it was like a cruise missile with wings. It went right there and slammed right into the Pentagon."

When *Popular Mechanics* contacted the journalist, he expressed dismay over the way Meyssan had manipulated his words. "I struggle with the fact that my comments will forever be taken out of context," says Walter, who sought counseling to alleviate post-traumatic stress disorder from witnessing the crash. "I don't know that it will ever go away."

Hundreds of morning commuters saw the plane as it made its low-level approach—dozens of them told reporters that they recognized it not only as a passenger jet but also as an American Airlines plane. To cite just one example, William Lagasse, a Pentagon police officer, told ABC's *Nightline*: "It was close enough that I could see the windows and the blinds had been pulled down. I read American Airlines on it . . . I saw the aircraft above my head about 80 feet above the ground."

In addition, at least two people aboard—flight attendant Renee May and passenger Barbara Olson, wife of solicitor general Ted Olson—phoned family members to let them know the plane had been hijacked. All but five of the 189 people who died on the aircraft and in the Pentagon were later identified through DNA testing. (The five hijackers were positively identified.) Author Meyssan has said that the plane was likely destroyed somewhere in Ohio. That was where the hijackers turned off the transponder at 8:56 a.m. and made a U-turn for the flight back to Washington D.C. However, he does not explain what happened to the wreckage or how the DNA of those on board was recovered in the Pentagon.

It is true that after the crash, only pieces of the plane were recovered: the landing gear and bits of the fuselage, among others. Much of the airliner was pulverized due to the combination of the plane's mass and velocity (see "Big Plane, Small Holes") and the dense interior structure of the Pentagon. "As the plane penetrated through the building, it was literally encountering a forest of columns. The plane disintegrated on itself," says Paul Mlakar, a senior research scientist with the U.S. Army Corps of Engineers, who was team leader for *The Pentagon Building Performance Report,* released in January 2003. The investigation, commissioned by the American Society of Civil Engineers (ASCE), was conducted by a team of experts to assess the structural performance of the building. As a rough comparison, Mlakar says the effect on the plane was "like taking a Coke can and smashing it against the wall. The back and the front become one."

The concrete columns ranged in width from 21 by 21 inches on the ground floor to 14 by 14 inches on the fifth floor and had recently been reinforced as part of the Pentagon's Renovation and Construction Program. (The building was a rush job completed in 1943 after only 16 months.) Budgeted at approximately $1.3 billion and slated to take 17 years, the modernization program started in 1993 and is considered to be the largest such project in the world.

Because of the violence of the crash and the fire that followed, photographs of the interior of the Pentagon show primarily charred heaps of rubble. As the conspiracy-friendly Web site www.rense.com notes, the photos reveal wreckage that is mostly stacked or wrapped around the support columns, an observation consistent with Mlakar's description of the crash. However, a small piece of the fuselage, with portions of the American Airlines logo visible, was photographed on the lawn in front of the Pentagon (see photo 22).

Within minutes of the crash, FBI agents arrived on the scene and began collecting that debris, including the piece of fuselage on the lawn. Many conspiracy theorists point to this as further evidence of a cover-up. However, airline accident experts say that is standard protocol because the multiple aircraft crashing at the same time under suspicious circumstances immediately indicated that the Pentagon was a crime scene. "Once it has been determined as a non-accident," says Matthew McCormick, retired chief of the Survival Factors Division of the National Transportation Safety Board, "then the FBI steps in and takes it over as a criminal event."

Just as the police wouldn't leave a murder weapon lying around in the grass, says McCormick, who worked on crash sites for 33 years, investigators commonly collect aircraft debris as quickly as possible to preserve the integrity of the evidence. Todd Curtis, a former airline safety analyst for Boeing and founder of AirSafe.com, says it was even more urgent than usual for the FBI to begin collecting evidence at the Pentagon because the large number of emergency personnel on the scene meant there was increased potential for first responders to inadvertently destroy or damage evidence of the crash.

Structural engineer Allyn E. Kilsheimer was one of those first responders. His reaction to doubters like Meyssan is visceral. "It was absolutely a plane, and I'll tell you why," says Kilsheimer, CEO of KCE Structural Engineers in Washington D.C. "I saw the marks of the plane wing on the face of the stone on one side of the building. I picked up parts of the plane with the airline markings on them. I held in my hand the tail section of the plane, and I stood on a pile of debris that we later discovered contained the black box. . . . I held parts of uniforms from crew members in my hands, including body parts. Okay?"

# Big Plane, Small Holes

**CLAIM:** Two holes were visible in the Pentagon immediately after the attack: a messy 90-foot gash in the building's exterior wall, and a round 16-foot-wide hole in Ring C, the Pentagon's middle ring. Conspiracy theorists argue that both holes are far too small to have been made by a Boeing 757. For years, www.reopen911.org, a Web site "dedicated to opening a real investigation into the tragic attacks on September 11, 2001," asked, "How does a plane 125 feet wide and 155 feet long fit into a hole which is only 16 feet across?" The question was subsequently picked up by numerous Web sites.

Reopen911.org is bankrolled by Jimmy Walter, heir to a Florida-based home-building fortune. In the December 7, 2005, edition of the *Tampa Tribune*, Walter claimed that he had spent $6 million trying to prove that the 9/11 attacks were actually part of a massive conspiracy. Walter's campaign to question the findings of the 9/11 Commission has included spot ads on cable networks (CNN, ESPN, and Fox News), as well as full-page ads in the *New York Times, Washington Post,* and *Newsweek*. In an open letter on his reopen911 Web site, Walter says, "It seems clear to me that someone executed a master of deception's plan and killed thousands of innocent people. Osama and Bush may just be patsies."

**FACT:** When Flight 77 hit the Pentagon it created a hole in the exterior wall of the building approximately 90 feet wide, according to *The Pentagon Building Performance Report*.

The report acknowledges that the width of the hole is approximate because the exterior facade collapsed 19 minutes after impact, obviously well before measurements could be made. The team based the estimate on the number and position of first-floor support columns that were destroyed or damaged near the point of impact. Engineers and computer scientists from Purdue University confirmed the findings through a detailed computer simulation of the crash. Using a bank of IBM supercomputers, the study involved nearly 275 hours of computation time for each second of the crash and its aftermath.

But the question remains: Why wasn't the initial hole as wide as a 757's 124-foot, 10-inch wingspan?

For one thing, both wings were damaged before striking the Pentagon facade. Pentagon employee Frank Probst was walking outside the building on his way to a 10 a.m. meeting as the plane approached; it was flying so low that Probst actually dove to the ground because he thought the plane might hit him. After the plane passed, Probst, a West Point graduate and decorated Vietnam War veteran, turned and saw the right wing smash into a portable 750-kilowatt generator that was set on a concrete pad outside the Pentagon. The massive generator provided backup power to Wedge 1, an area of about 1 million square feet that housed 5,000 Pentagon employees. Probst also saw the left engine strike a ground-level external vent positioned just outside the exterior wall of the Pentagon.

Probst's observations are bolstered by one of his colleagues, Don Mason, who was stuck in traffic just west of the Pentagon and who saw the plane clip three light poles on its approach. He watched Probst dive to the ground and then saw a small explosion when the right wing hit the portable generator.

The tips of the wings are farthest from an airplane's center of gravity and are therefore relatively fragile. As a result, it appears that the outer portions of both wings sheared off in the precrash collisions, says Paul Mlakar, team leader for the ASCE study. The study is not entirely conclusive because the collisions occurred within a split second of the plane reaching the Pentagon: Some investigators initially believed one of the wings hit the ground before impact and Mlakar acknowledges it is also possible that portions of the wings closer to the fuselage were sheared off upon striking the building. "Some portion of each wing was likely removed in the impacts before the facade," Mlakar says. "The remaining portions likely did not penetrate significantly beyond the facade."

However the damage to the wings was caused, it minimized the destruction in another important way: At the time of impact, an estimated 80 percent of the plane's 5,324 gallons of fuel was stored in the wings, at least one fifth of which never entered the building. According to *The Pentagon Building Performance Report,* most of the fuel ignited upon impact; the large fireball outside the building burned off about 700 gallons of fuel. This obviously lessened the amount of fire damage to the interior. And, the fuel that did enter the building traveled a maximum of 310 feet along the ground floor of a five-story building, and burned there. This is in stark contrast to the World Trade Center towers, where thousands of gallons of fuel penetrated the buildings' central structures, ignited, and ultimately weakened the buildings, leading to their collapse.

In any event, a jet doesn't punch a cartoonlike outline into a concrete building upon impact, says Mete Sozen, the Kettelhut Distinguished Professor of Civil Engineering at Purdue University. According to Sozen, who was one of four civil engineers that ASCE sent to study the damage to the Pentagon, the energy load of a plane—not its shape or structure—is the critical factor determining its effect on a building in a crash. This was revealed in Purdue's computer simulation, which adapted software typically used to evaluate auto crashes to the scenario of a 757 airplane, the mass of which is mostly fluid fuel, traveling at 531 miles per hour and striking a building filled with reinforced concrete columns. Sozen says the resulting energy load rendered the exterior of the plane "like a sausage skin" that crumbled upon impact. What was left of the plane flowed into the structure in a state closer to a liquid than a solid mass, a phenomenon hinted at by eyewitness Penny Elgas, a federal administrative supervisor. Like Mason, Elgas was stuck in traffic near the Pentagon and watched the crash unfold. The plane, she said, "seemed to simply melt into the building."

What about the neat 16-foot hole in Ring C? (For the record, Mlakar tells *Popular Mechanics* the hole was closer to 15 feet wide.) The Web site www.the7thfire.com, run by a former science and social studies teacher who claims to "bridge worlds of thought and being, science and shamanism," asks: "Can you imagine something in an aluminum aircraft that could remain intact through six walls, multiple pillars and leave an exit wound so small?" The site goes on to say that the hole could not have been created by an engine or the aircraft's nose and therefore must have been caused by a missile.

In fact, the hole was not made by an engine or the nose of Flight 77 pushing through the building's interior—or a missile—but by the crashing jet's landing gear, which was ejected beyond the bulk of the wreckage. Because of the physical properties noted by Sozen, the less dense items, including the shell of the plane and the bodies of those on board, essentially disintegrated upon impact. The impact, however, also created a hole through which the heavier, denser items could continue forward into the building. The flight data recorder, for example, which was originally located near the back of the plane, was found almost 300 feet inside the building, considerably beyond where much of the wreckage from the front of the plane came to rest.

As one of the heaviest and most dense parts of the plane, the landing gear flew farther than any other item in the wreckage and was responsible for puncturing the wall in Ring C. Mlakar said he saw the landing gear with his own eyes, as did Paul Carlton Jr., surgeon general of the Air Force.

"I thought it was a terrorist bomb," Carlton told Dean Murphy in his book, *September 11: An Oral History.* "But then I saw the landing gear. It was on the ground in the alley between the B and C rings. When I saw it there, not only did I realize an airplane had struck the Pentagon but it was clear that the plane had come through the E, D, and C buildings to get there."

# Intact Pentagon Windows

**CLAIM:** Many of the Pentagon windows remained in one piece—even those just above the point of impact from the Boeing 757 passenger plane. The animation on www.pentagonstrike.co.uk claims the "intact windows" support the theory that "a missile" or "a craft much smaller than a 757" hit the Pentagon.

**FACT:** A number of windows near the impact area did indeed survive the initial concussion and ensuing explosion, because that's exactly what they were designed to do—the windows in that section of the Pentagon are blast-resistant.

The windows were installed just weeks earlier as part of a massive Pentagon modernization plan. The original windows were essentially standard commercial units from the early 1940s. The need for blast protection in the E and A rings—the outermost and innermost rings, respectively—became clear after the bombings of the Alfred P. Murrah Federal Building in Oklahoma City in 1995 and the embassies in Kenya and Tanzania in 1998.

In a rare stroke of good luck on September 11, Flight 77 struck Wedge 1, the first section of the building designated for renovation. That first phase was five days from completion when the plane hit, and 383 new-and-improved windows were already in place. Weighing approximately 1,600 pounds apiece, the new windows feature laminated glass, in which a thin polymer interlayer is sandwiched between two or more panes of glass. The effect is that the windows will crack but not shatter, much like a car windshield. Because the Pentagon was designated a National Historic Landmark in 1992, the new windows were required to match the exterior look of the originals, so it is impossible to tell the old from the new from the outside.

But installing new windows would not have made much of a difference without corresponding structural improvements in the building around them. As a result, the designers engineered a complicated reinforcement scheme with steel beams built into the walls around the window frames and bolted to the concrete floor slabs. The structure behaves like a catcher's mitt, absorbing the force of an explosion and shielding the people inside the building.

"It would be imprudent and sort of counterproductive to have a window that was stronger than the wall," says Ken Hays, executive vice president of Masonry Arts, the Bessemer, Alabama-based company that designed, manufactured, and installed the windows. "The wall should be stronger than the window glass. If the window construction is stronger than the wall, it would eject the window from the unit and now you've got a flying missile. You want to design your windows and structure so that they fail in a certain order."

Hays declined to discuss the levels of force the Pentagon windows are designed to withstand, as doing so could jeopardize the security of the building. However, he says, the windows performed to specifications. "I personally inspected those windows, and anywhere a window was not actually hit by the fuselage of the aircraft, the best we were able to determine was that if there was glass missing, it was because the subsequent fire burned the glass out."

Bill Hopper, communications manager for the Pentagon Renovation and Construction Program, confirms this account. *The Pentagon Building Performance Report* adds that the reinforcement around the windows kept the edifice surrounding the impact hole standing for 19 minutes. That was long enough to enable hundreds of Pentagon employees to exit the building before the damaged section of Ring E collapsed.

If the plane had hit an unrenovated section of the building, the damage would have been much more severe—not only from the force of the blast, but also from fire. In Wedge 1, where a new high-tech sprinkler system had been installed during the renovation, the fires did not spread significantly and most were put out fairly quickly. When some fires spread to Wedge 2, which did not have an upgraded sprinkler system, they burned on and off for more than 24 hours.

# 5

# FLIGHT 93

Scheduled for an 8 a.m. departure, United Airlines Flight 93 took off with 37 passengers from Newark's Liberty International Airport 25 minutes late due to heavy runway traffic on the morning of September 11, 2001. It was the only one of the four targeted flights that was significantly delayed. The terrorist plot entailed taking four airplanes almost simultaneously, then crashing them before the authorities could understand and react to what was happening. But because of the delay in Newark, Flight 93 became airborne just four minutes before American Airlines Flight 11 hit the North Tower of the World Trade Center.

At 9:28 a.m., 25 minutes after United Airlines Flight 175 crashed into the South Tower, a Cleveland air traffic controller assigned to Flight 93 heard signs of a struggle in the cockpit, followed shortly by screaming. At 9:39 a.m., hijacker pilot Ziad Jarrah transmitted this message: "Uh, this is the captain. Would like you all to remain seated. There is a bomb on board and are going back to the airport." The 9/11 Commission believes Jarrah thought he was talking to

A growing army of conspiracy theorists insists that the 9/11 attacks were not committed by Islamist terrorists affiliated with Al Qaeda. They argue instead that the U.S. government was somehow complicit in the attacks. Seizing flimsy evidence, theorists charge that the World Trade Center buildings were professionally demolished; a missile or military jet—not a Boeing 757—struck the Pentagon; Flight 93 was hit by an air-to-air missile before it crashed in Pennsylvania; and American air defenses were ordered to "stand down" on 9/11. In November 2004, *Popular Mechanics,* a magazine with more than 100 years of experience reporting on engineering, aviation, civil defense, and related fields, launched an investigation into these claims. For this book, the magazine's reporters interviewed more than 300 experts and examined a wide array of evidence before concluding that none of the theorists' claims stands up to scrutiny.

# THE PLANES

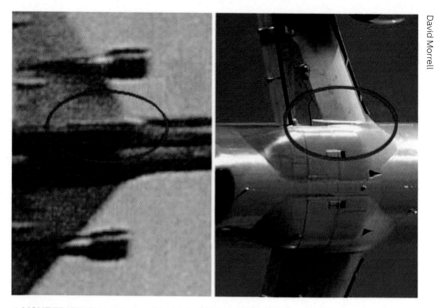

David Morrell

**1. LIGHT TRICK:** Some photos of the United Airlines Flight 175 (above, left) appear to show a bulge in the fuselage at the base of the Boeing 767's right wing. Some theorists speculate that this could be a "military pod" or missile. Experts say the photo is distorted by sunlight and that the bulge is, in fact, the plane's right fairing, which holds the landing gear, as seen in the photograph of an identical Boeing 767 (above, right).

**2. PLAIN VIEW:**
One eyewitness reported that the plane that hit WTC 2 did not have any windows, leading to speculation that it could have been a military cargo plane or fuel tanker. This photo of aircraft debris on the roof of WTC 5 includes a section of fuselage that clearly had passenger windows.

William F. Baker/FEMA

Many conspiracy theorists question how four amateur pilots could fly four jets across long distances into stationary targets. In fact, all four men were licensed private pilots and three held commercial licenses, which require at least 250 hours of air training. Aviation experts say taking off, landing, and flying through inclement weather are by far the most difficult aspects of flying. On 9/11, the terrorists did not have to do any of these things.

**3. MOHAMED ATTA:** A 33-year-old Egyptian and the oldest of the hijacker pilots, Atta was the leader of the attack group once all members were in the United States. He graduated from the Accelerated Pilot Program at Huffman Aviation International in Florida in August 2000 and received his commercial pilot's license in December. He failed his first instrument rating test but passed on the second try. He also trained in a jet simulator. Atta pilots American Airlines Flight 11 into the North Tower.

**4. HANI HANJOUR:** The most experienced pilot of the four and the only Saudi, Hanjour, 29, obtained his private pilot's license and commercial pilot's license in Arizona in 1999 before returning to the Middle East. He was recruited for the plot when Al Qaeda leaders learned he was a pilot. When Hanjour returned to Arizona in late 2000, he entered refresher training and Boeing 737 simulator training. Hanjour piloted American Airlines Flight 77 into the Pentagon.

**5. ZIAD JARRAH:** A native of Lebanon, Jarrah, 26, began training in the summer of 2000 at the Florida Flight Training Center and lived with flight instructors from the school. He received a private pilot's license in August 2000. He interrupted his flight training to take repeated trips abroad and never completed his commercial pilot's training. Jarrah was flying United Airlines Flight 93, which crashed in a field outside Shanksville, in southwestern Pennsylvania.

**6. MARWAN AL SHEHHI:** At 24, Shehhi was the youngest of the four hijacker pilots. He completed his early training with Atta, receiving a private pilot's certificate in Venice, Florida, as well as a commercial pilot's license in December 2000. A native of the United Arab Emirates, he spoke little English and often followed Atta's lead. Along with Atta, he rented several small planes for long practice flights in late 2000. Shehhi flew United Airlines Flight 175 into the South Tower.

# THE WORLD TRADE CENTER

**7. GAPING HOLE:** Conspiracy theorists claim that only a controlled demolition could have brought down the World Trade Center towers. But this photograph of WTC 1 (North Tower) shows that nearly half of the north face's exterior structural columns were severed by American Airlines Flight 11. This extensive damage to the towers, along with subsequent fires that weakened the steel frames, combined to bring down both WTC towers.

**8. BEFORE THE FALL:** This photo was taken on June 30, 2000 by Space Imaging Inc's IKONOS satellite, and shows a bird's-eye view of the World Trade Center site. Debris from the North Tower (WTC 1) damaged the south side of nearby WTC 7. According to NIST's final report, WTC 7's collapse was the cause of long-burning fires in the building's interior.

**9. FIRE ZONE:** A common observation made by conspiracy theorists is that numerous steel-frame buildings have undergone extensive fires yet remained standing. However, engineers and fire experts note that those buildings did not suffer the one-two punch of physical damage from the airplane crashes and prolonged exposure of structural steel to the resulting fires, the combination of which fatally compromised the WTC towers.

**10. BOWING STEEL:** Conspiracy theorists claim that fuel from the hijacked jets didn't burn hot enough or long enough to cause structural failure. Vertical lines on this photo of WTC 2's east face indicate the original line of vertical columns, while the small perpendicular bars show an inward bowing of about 10 inches just 18 minutes after the impact of Flight 175. WTC 1's south face was bowed inward some 55 inches six minutes before collapse.

**11. DUST PLUMES:** As each tower collapsed, horizontal plumes of dust and debris were ejected from the sides of the buildings, which some conspiracy theorists claim proves the existence of "squibs"—small electronic or pyrotechnic explosives used to ignite demolition charges. Structural engineers and other experts explain that the towers' "pancaking" floors created high air pressure in the structures and expelled air and debris out of the windows.

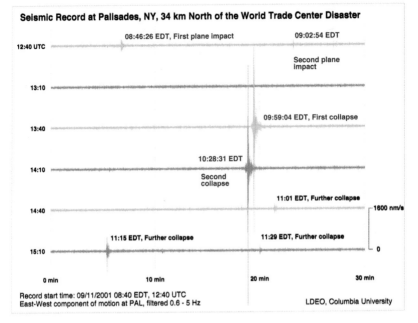

**Seismic Record at Palisades, NY, 34 km North of the World Trade Center Disaster**

08:46:26 EDT, First plane impact    09:02:54 EDT

12:40 UTC

Second plane impact

13:10

09:59:04 EDT, First collapse

13:40

10:28:31 EDT

14:10

Second collapse

11:01 EDT, Further collapse

14:40    — 1600 nm/s

11:15 EDT, Further collapse    11:29 EDT, Further collapse

15:10    — 0

0 min    10 min    20 min    30 min

Record start time: 09/11/2001 08:40 EDT, 12:40 UTC
East-West component of motion at PAL, filtered 0.6 - 5 Hz

LDEO, Columbia University

**12. 30-MINUTE GRAPH:** Seismographs at Columbia University's Lamont-Doherty Earth Observatory, 21 miles north of the World Trade Center, recorded two sharp spikes (above) as World Trade Center buildings collapsed on September 11. Conspiracy theorists say the spikes on this graph, which covers a 30-minute time frame, prove that bombs from a "demolition-style implosion" toppled the WTC 1 and WTC 2.

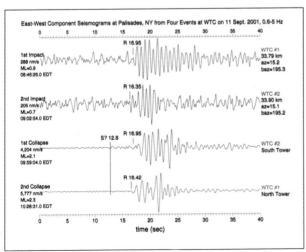

East-West Component Seismograms at Palisades, NY from Four Events at WTC on 11 Sept. 2001, 0.6-5 Hz

**13. 40-SECOND GRAPH:** Lamont-Doherty scientists say that on the 30-minute graph, the collapses appear—misleadingly—as sharp spikes. This 40-second plot of the same data gives a much more detailed picture: The seismic waves start small and then escalate as the two buildings rumble to the ground, showing no evidence of explosions.

**14. GRAVITY:** Some conspiracy theorists insist that the near-free-fall collapses of the World Trade Center towers signal controlled demolitions, but this photo illustrates ejected debris preceding the North Tower to the ground. The tower came down in about 10 seconds at an estimated speed of about 125 miles per hour. In a free fall, with no resistance, its collapse would have taken just over 9 seconds. The photo also shows the proximity of WTC 7—the tallest building in the center of the photo. WTC 7 sustained heavy damage from debris. That damage, along with fierce fires, brought down the building some seven hours after the towers fell.

**15. FIRESTORM:** WTC 7 endured fires that raged for up to seven hours. The fires caused the thermal expansion of key structural members in the tower, leading to its collapse.

**16. WTC 7 DAMAGE:** Conspiracy theorists claim that a controlled demolition leveled WTC 7, citing a preliminary FEMA report that the building and, until September 11, no steel skyscraper had ever collapsed because of a fire. A more extensive investigation by the National Institute of Standards and Technology showed that fires and damage from the collapse of the Twin Towers were far more extensive that originally believed.

The 102-story Empire State Building, shown here on January 1, 1945, was the first New York skyscraper to be struck by an airplane. Seven months later, a U.S. Army Air Corps B-25 slammed into the 79th floor in a heavy fog. Theorists ask why the landmark still stands, while the WTC towers fell in 56 minutes (South Tower) and 102 minutes (North Tower).

### 17. BUILT TOUGH:
The Empire State Building has a heavy steel frame, with beams encased in fire-proofing concrete. During construction, WTC steel was sprayed with a fire-resistant foam, which was knocked off by the planes' impact.

### 18. FATAL FORCE:
The B-25 was one-tenth the size of a 767. The bomber hit the 79th floor at about 200 miles per hour, punching an 18- by 20-foot hole. The hijacked 767s were flying at 440 miles per hour (North Tower) and 540 miles per hour (South Tower), and destroyed multiple floors in the WTC.

### 19. LOBBY FIRES:
Some of the bomber's 800 gallons of fuel ignited on impact, and an unknown amount flowed down elevator shafts, igniting fires in the lobby (shown here). The 767s on 9/11 had about 10,000 gallons of fuel, some of which also poured down elevator shafts.

# THE PENTAGON

**20. CRIME SCENE:** Taken on September 14, 2001, this photo shows the extent of the damage to the Pentagon, consistent with a fiery plane crash. French author Thierry Meyssan says the hole in the Pentagon facade is too small for a plane and must have been caused by a missile. In fact, the plane's wings were likely sheared off prior to impact; engineering experts say a crashing jet wouldn't be expected to punch a cartoonlike outline of itself into a reinforced concrete building, but to flow into it in a fluidlike manner.

**21. RING E:** Some conspiracy theorists say the intact windows near the point of impact support the missile theory, arguing that a plane crash would have knocked them out. But the recently installed windows were blast-resistant and performed as designed. This is one of the few photos taken of the facade before it collapsed.

**22. LAWN DEBRIS:**
Conspiracy theorists question why pieces of Flight 77 were not visible in the wreckage and conclude that it was not a plane that struck the Pentagon. Experts say most of the plane disintegrated inside the building; this photo shows a small piece of the Flight 77's fuselage on the Pentagon lawn.

**23. EXIT WOUND:**
This 15-foot hole in Ring C of the Pentagon was not caused by a missile, but the plane's landing gear, which was thrown forward in the crash. A portion of the charred landing gear is visible between the fire hose and the fireman's back.

# FLIGHT 93

SSGT Greg L. Davis, USAF

**24. MISSING TARGETS:** F–16s like these from the North Dakota Air National Guard were unable to intercept the hijacked planes before they crashed, leading some to contend the military was ordered to "stand down" on September 11. The reality: Only 14 fighters were on alert that morning in the Lower 48; interceptions of civilian aircraft rarely occurred over the continental U.S. and when the hijackers turned off their transponders the missing planes were extremely difficult to track in some of the country's busiest air lanes.

International Mapping

**25. INDIAN LAKE:** Theorists claim that debris found in Indian Lake was six miles from the crash site. Their interpretation: The plane was breaking up prior to impact and was therefore shot down. The lake is six miles from the crash site by road, but it is only 1.5 miles geographically. Experts say it is not surprising that light crash debris blew there.

**26. HEROES' END:** Flight 93 was flying 580 miles per hour when it crashed in southwestern Pennsylvania, gouging a 30-foot-deep crater into the earth on impact and obliterating most of the wreckage. Some conspiracy theorists claim an engine was found miles away, indicating to them that a heat-seeking missile brought down the airliner. The engine was actually found downhill from the crash site, 300 yards away.

**27. FLIGHT DATA:** The contents of the so-called black box of United Airlines Flight 93 (shown here) refute conspiracy theories that the plane was shot down. In April 2006, the tape was played in public for the first time during the sentencing trial of Zacarias Moussaoul, who pleaded guilty to terrorism conspiracy and was sentenced to life in prison. Three minutes before the crash, a voice in Arabic asks, "Is that it? Shall we finish it off?" Two minutes later, a voice in Arabic says, "Pull it down. Pull it down." The tape concludes with voices saying repeatedly, "Allah is the greatest."

ASSAULT ON THE TRUTH: Ten years after 9/11, conspiracy theories continue to proliferate. *Popular Mechanics'* investigation has shown that, without exception, the facts cited by conspiracy theorists in support of their views are incorrect, misinterpreted, or falsified. There is overwhelming evidence that Al Qaeda planned and carried out the attacks. Although the U.S. government was woefully ineffective in dealing with the threat, claims that shadowy elements within it conspired to attack American citizens are without foundation.

the passengers, but was actually speaking to the Cleveland controller.

The Federal Aviation Administration had as much as 35 minutes to alert the military that a fourth plane had been hijacked. Yet because of miscommunication and the lack of a protocol for this scenario, fighters were not sent to intercept Flight 93 while it was in the air. As on the other hijacked flights, passengers used seat-back air phones and, intermittently, cell phones to contact loved ones. Because of the take-off delay, they alone among the hijacked passengers were able to learn that America was under attack by terrorists who were seizing commercial airliners. In a phone call to his wife 18 minutes before the crash, medical-device executive Tom Burnett told her that he and other passengers were planning to take back the plane, or perhaps preempt the terrorists' plans. "If they're going to crash this plane into the ground, we're going to have to do something," Burnett said. Other passengers, including Todd Beamer and Jeremy Glick, also told loved ones that they were planning to attack the hijackers.

At 10:03 a.m., Flight 93 plowed into a field outside Shanksville in southwestern Pennsylvania. The 9/11 Commission reports that the terrorists originally intended for Jarrah to fly the plane into the U.S. Capitol. The cockpit recording recovered from the crash site indicates that passengers did attack the hijackers, although it is not clear who actually forced the plane to the ground. In the last moments, one hijacker tells another in Arabic to "pull it down" and later repeats "Allah is the greatest" until the recording ends.

As a result of their actions, the Flight 93 passengers were widely hailed as heroes, and celebrated in best-selling books and *United 93*, which debuted in April 2006 as the number one movie in the country.

But conspiracy theorists see a more sinister tale: They assert that Flight 93 was destroyed by a heat-seeking missile fired by an F-16 or a mysterious white plane. Other theorists claim that there were no terrorists on board, or that the passengers were drugged. Still others believe that the many phone calls from passengers to family members and other acquaintances were faked. The conspirators, theorists say, used elaborate voice modification technology to make the call recipients believe they were talking to loved ones when, in fact, government agents were on the other end of the call.

The most elaborate scenario is the "bumble planes" theory, which holds that passengers from Flights 11 and 175, as well as from Flight 77, which crashed into the Pentagon, were loaded onto Flight 93 so the U.S. government could kill them. A less overheated, but still troubling, theory holds that the U.S. government shot down the plane and then covered it up to avoid upsetting the American public.

# F-16 Pilot

**CLAIM:** In February 2004, self-described retired Army Colonel Donn de Grand-Pre said on *The Alex Jones Show*, a radio talk show broadcast across the country, that he knew what happened to Flight 93: "It was taken out by the North Dakota Air Guard," he said. "I know the pilot who fired those two missiles to take down 93." He goes on to say that the pilot was a member of a unit in the guard known as the Happy Hooligans. The Web site, www.letsroll911.org, citing Grand-Pre, later identified the pilot: "Major Rick Gibney fired two Sidewinder missiles at the aircraft and destroyed it in midflight at precisely 0958."

In the radio interview, Grand-Pre also boasts that he contacted his "friend" General Hugh Shelton, who was chairman of the Joint Chiefs of Staff at the time, about his concerns. He says his 24-page report outlining what really happened on 9/11 was subsequently distributed widely within the military and even passed on to the White House.

**FACT:** Four fighters from the 119th Fighter Wing, which calls itself the Happy Hooligans, were at Langley Air Force Base outside Washington D.C. for a training mission on September 11, 2001, but Gibney was not one of the pilots. Gibney (the operations group commander and a lieutenant colonel, not a major), was at the unit's home base in Fargo, North Dakota.

On the morning of September 11, the National Emergency Management Association was conducting its annual conference, in Big Sky, Montana. Soon after the attacks on the World Trade Center and the Pentagon, an Air Force transport plane was dispatched to pick up Joe Allbaugh, then director of the Federal Emergency Management Agency, and other top FEMA officials and fly them to Washington D.C. Edward Jacoby Jr., director of the New York State Emergency Management Office, similarly needed to get back to his home state as quickly as possible. Gibney was assigned to fly him there in a two-seat F-16B; the fighter was unarmed.

Air National Guard public information officer Master Sergeant David E. Somdahl says flight records show that Gibney took off from Fargo at 10:45 a.m. eastern daylight time to pick up Jacoby in Bozeman, Montana—42 minutes after Flight 93 crashed in Shanksville, Pennsylvania. Fargo is more than 1,100 miles northwest of Shanksville, making it impossible for Gibney to have shot down Flight 93 and returned to Fargo in time to make the Fargo departure. Departing Bozeman at 3:30 p.m. eastern daylight time, Gibney flew Jacoby to Albany, New York, so Jacoby could coordinate 17,000 rescue workers engaged in the state's response to 9/11. The two men arrived in the New York state capital at 6:30 p.m. An hour and 20 minutes later, Gibney flew to Langley, arriving at 8:50 p.m. Saying he was reluctant to fuel debate by responding to unsubstantiated charges, Gibney declined to comment.

Jacoby confirms the day's events. He is outraged by the claim that Gibney shot down Flight 93. "I summarily dismiss that because Lieutenant Colonel Gibney was with me at that time. It disgusts me to see this because the public is being misled," Jacoby tells *Popular Mechanics*. Jacoby returned to North Dakota to present Gibney and other members of the Happy Hooligans with awards for their service on September 11. (Conspiracy theorists claim that Gibney's citation was a reward for his role in shooting down Flight 93.)

Somdahl says he is familiar with Grand-Pre's allegations. "I know he claims he knows our pilots, which is false. I know he claims he knows our adjutant general, which is false," he says. "I know everything he has claimed about Lieutenant Colonel Rick Gibney and the 119th Fighter Wing is complete crap."

General Shelton, who is now retired, also refutes Grand-Pre's claims. "I don't know this individual," Shelton tells *Popular Mechanics*. "The name doesn't ring a bell and I certainly never saw any report that he rendered alleging there was some type of conspiracy or that a National Guard pilot shot down [Flight 93]." That's no surprise: Deeper research reveals that Grand-Pre, whom conspiracists alternately affiliate with the Army and the Marine Corp, was in fact a Colonel—in the Army National Guard. A reader of the blog Screw Loose Change (www.screwloosechange.blogspot. com) reached out to the POW Network for a copy of Grand-Pre's military records, which include service from 1944-46, and again from 1951-56. His career was largely spent in civil affairs. Shelton continues: "I have a reputation for being candid, and if I had seen a paper like that or heard a story like that, I would tell you, and I would tell you what I did with it. I never heard anything that was anything close to what he was saying. From my perspective, all that is hogwash."

As to whether another fighter could have shot down the plane, the 9/11 Commission report is clear that no shoot-down order was in place for Flight 93, due to garbled communication between the various agencies. When the flight crashed, NORAD was still unaware the plane had been hijacked. At approximately 10:02 a.m.—a minute before Flight 93 crashed—the FAA notified the Secret Service about a hijacked aircraft bound for Washington D.C. The Secret Service asked Vice President Dick Cheney, who was in contact with President Bush, for permission to shoot down any remaining hijacked aircraft. Cheney was in the

White House shelter conference room while Bush was in Florida; the two men discussed the situation over the phone. Cheney told the 9/11 Commission that Bush authorized the shoot-down order, which Cheney then gave to a military aide between 10:12 a.m. and 10:18 a.m.—after Flight 93 had crashed. The first written record of the shoot-down order came at 10:20 a.m., when White House press secretary Ari Fleischer, traveling with President Bush, made a note aboard Air Force One.

The details of the communication between the FAA and the military on 9/11 are still under investigation by the Departments of Transportation and Defense. However, the shoot-down protocol was changed immediately following 9/11: The president delegated shoot-down responsibility to several top NORAD generals, so that in a tactical situation in which they believe a shoot-down is necessary, they have the authority to order one. Meanwhile, the FAA, NORAD, and approximately 80 other government agencies now have access to the Domestic Events Network, a 24-hour conference line that informs all groups of unfolding events.

# The White Jet

**CLAIM:** Flight 93 was shot down by a mysterious white jet. At least six eyewitnesses say they saw a small white jet flying low over the crash area almost immediately after Flight 93 went down. The political blog www.blogd.com theorizes that "the plane was brought down, not by a struggle, but on orders from the government. Either a missile fired from an Air Force jet, or via an electronic assault made by a U.S. Customs airplane reported to have been seen near the site minutes after flight 93 crashed." The site www.worldnetdaily.com, run by former newspaper journalist Joseph Farah, finds the allegation credible: "Witnesses to this low-flying jet came forward and told their story to journalists. . . . Shortly thereafter, the FBI began to attack the witnesses with perhaps the most inane disinformation ever—alleging the witnesses actually observed a private jet at 34,000 feet. The FBI says the jet was asked to come down to 5,000 feet and try to find the crash site. This would require about 20 minutes to descend."

**FACT:** There was such a jet in the vicinity—a Dassault Falcon 20 business jet owned by the VF Corporation, an apparel company that markets Wrangler, The North Face, and other brands. The eight-passenger VF plane (mostly white with gold markings) was flying from the company's headquarters in Greensboro, North Carolina, to Johnstown, Pennsylvania, where the company had a manufacturing facility at the time. The Johnstown-Cambria airport is 20 miles north of Shanksville.

According to David Newell, VF's director of aviation and travel, the FAA's Cleveland Center contacted copilot Yates Gladwell when the Falcon was at an altitude "in the neighborhood of 3,000 to 4,000 feet"—not 34,000 feet. "They were in a descent already going into Johnstown," Newell adds. "The FAA asked them to investigate and they did. They got down within 1,500 feet of the ground when they circled.

They saw a hole in the ground with smoke coming out of it."
Newell says the plane circled the crash site twice and then
flew directly over it in order to mark the exact latitude and
longitude on the plane's navigation system.

Reached by *Popular Mechanics*, Gladwell confirmed
this account. Concerned about ongoing harassment by
conspiracy theorists, he asked not to be quoted directly.

Newell says he has received dozens of calls from people
who want to ask him about the company jet's activities on
September 11. "There's nothing to hide," he says. "But the
vast majority of them want to make out some kind of story
that's just not there."

# Cell-Phone Calls

**CLAIM:**    Much of what we know about what happened on Flight 93 comes from cell-phone
calls made by passengers and crew in the 47 minutes between
the hijacking and the plane's crash. This is strange since
"given the prevailing technology in September 2001, it was
extremely difficult, if not impossible, to place a wireless cell
call from an aircraft traveling at high speed above 8,000 feet,"
writes Michael Chossudovsky on the Web site for the Centre
for Research on Globalization, www.globalresearch.ca. The
Quebec-based nonprofit describes itself as an independent
research group that has become a "major news source on the
New World Order." In Chossudovsky's view, the impossibil-
ity of cell-phone calls proves that at least part of the 9/11
Commission's report is "fabricated."

In an article on the Web site www.physics911.net, A. K. Dewdney also raises questions about the calls. The professor emeritus of computer science theorizes that the calls must have been "staged" because "cell-phone calls from commercial aircraft much over 8000 feet are essentially impossible, while those below 8000 feet are highly unlikely."

**FACT:** While not exactly reliable, cell-phone calls from airplanes were possible in 2001—even from extremely high altitudes. "Because cell sites have a range of several miles, even at 35,000 feet, that's entirely possible," says Rick Kemper, director of technology and security at the CTIA—The Wireless Association. "It's not a very good connection, and it changes a lot, and you end up getting a lot of dropped calls because you're moving through cell sites so fast."

Paul Guckian, vice president of engineering for cell-phone maker Qualcomm, concurs. "I would say that at the altitude for commercial airliners, around 30,000 or 35,000 feet, [some] phones would still get a signal," he tells *Popular Mechanics*. "At some point above that—I would estimate in the 50,000-foot range—you would lose the signal." Flight 93 never flew higher than 40,700 feet.

Of course, it has long been against FAA regulations to use cell phones on planes. There are two reasons: One is that airborne calls can on occasion interfere with planes' navigation and communication systems. This is the reason cited by flight attendants when they ask passengers to turn off phones prior to takeoff. The other, less widely known reason is that a single airborne call might be picked up by multiple cell towers on the ground. This confuses the system and can result in dropped calls across the network. As a result, the Federal Communications Commission has been a strong supporter of the ban on in-flight cell-phone calls. (Several manufacturers have announced plans to release systems that circumvent these problems.)

Many factors are involved in a successful cell-phone connection. When the phone is turned on, it searches for the strongest signal from a nearby tower. As the customer moves farther away from the tower, the signal gets weaker and the phone and the tower negotiate a "handoff" to another tower with a stronger signal. The network routinely manages handoffs at car speeds, but it struggles to make the high-speed handoffs required when the customer is in an airplane traveling more than 400 miles per hour.

The altitude of the plane is also a factor. The lower the plane is flying, the closer it is to cell-phone towers. A less-obvious factor is population density: Towers in urban areas cover as little as one square mile each, while rural towers may cover several hundred square miles. This means passengers in planes traveling over rural areas can stick with a signal for a longer period of time without getting dropped during a high-speed handoff.

At least 10 passengers and two crew members contacted loved ones or colleagues on the ground from Flight 93—the most of any of the hijacked planes. Some used seat-back air phones, but several made calls via cell phones. The plane's generally low altitude and the rural terrain below may have contributed to the cell calls going through.

The calls that did connect were brief. On Flight 93, passenger Tom Burnett called his wife three times from his cell phone; each communication lasted less than a minute. According to *New York Times* reporter Jere Longman's book about Flight 93, *Among the Heroes*, passengers Lauren Grandcolas and Mark Bingham also made short cell-phone calls to friends and family. There is also evidence of calls cutting off, such as passenger Andrew Garcia, whose call ended after he uttered his wife's name, Dorothy.

The other 9/11 planes each contained five hijackers; Flight 93 was commandeered by just four men, which may have contributed to the high number of calls. As two callers from the flight reported, the hijackers didn't seem to mind passengers making calls. "Perhaps, with so few hijackers trying to control so many passengers," Longman writes, "the terrorists considered it too risky to intervene. Perhaps the passengers in the rear of the plane were being only loosely watched, or were left unattended."

With 33 hijacked passengers on board and apparently easy access to phones, it seems likely that others tried to make calls but could not get through.

Flight attendant CeeCee Lyles made one of the last calls. A former police officer with two sons and two stepsons, she called her husband, Lorne, by cell phone at 9:58 a.m., shortly after passengers began storming the cockpit. Her name registered in the family's caller ID readout. Lorne Lyles picked up, and prayed with his wife until he heard screaming and what he described as a "whooshing sound, a sound like wind," Longman writes. The call then broke off.

# The Wreckage

**CLAIM:** One of Flight 93's engines was found "at a considerable distance from the crash site," according to Lyle Szupinka, a state police officer on the scene who was quoted in the *Pittsburgh Tribune-Review*. In an article sympathetic to a variety of Flight 93 conspiracy theories, the August 13, 2002, edition of the London tabloid *The Independent* puts the distance at more than a mile from the main crater, suggesting that the plane was coming apart prior to impact. Why is that significant? It backs up the contention that Flight 93 was shot down. As a post on www.rense.com puts it, "The main body of the engine of Flight 93 was found miles away from the main wreckage site, with damage comparable to that which a heat-seeking missile would do to an airliner."

The Web site www.september11news.com, which explores what it calls "9/11 mysteries," expresses other concerns about the crash site: "Why are there no known pictures available of the Flight 93 wreckage? The only pictures show rescue workers peering into a crater, but there is no wreckage to be seen."

**FACT:** A fan from one of the engines was recovered in the catchment basin of a small pond downhill from the crash site. According to Jeff Reinbold, the National Park Service representative responsible for the Flight 93 National Memorial, the basin is 300 yards from the impact crater. That is less than a fifth of a mile—not more than a mile and certainly not "miles away."

The fan was one of the largest surviving pieces of the plane. Most of the aircraft was obliterated on impact, shattering into tiny pieces that were driven as much as 30 feet into the earth. Rick King of the Shanksville Fire Department, who was one of the first on the scene, told Charles Gibson of ABC News, "When I got there, I wondered to myself, 'Where is it?' The plane was just totally disintegrated."

Greg Feith, a former senior investigator with the National Transportation Safety Board (NTSB), says this is a typical outcome when a plane hits the ground at high speed. Most crashes occur at takeoff or landing, when the speed of the plane is relatively slow. "You can liken crash debris to an egg. At a slow speed, dropped from your hand, the impact will crack the egg and you'll have large pieces of shell," Feith tells *Popular Mechanics*. "Take an egg and drop it from 20 stories up and it will have smaller fragments of shell."

So it's not that there are no pictures of the Flight 93 wreckage—there simply was very little wreckage to show (see photo 26). Feith recalls a 1997 crash he investigated on the Indonesian island of Sumatra. In a suspected pilot suicide, the plane went into a nosedive from 35,000 feet. It actually reached the speed of sound—about 761 miles per hour at sea level—before plunging into the Musi River. At that crash site, Feith says, investigators found little more than a tire carcass and engine parts the size of a pot lid.

By comparison, Flight 93 turned sharply to the right in its final moments, rolling onto its back. It collided with the Shanksville field at approximately 580 miles per hour, traveling south-southeast at a steep, but not vertical, angle.

Feith says it is significant that the plane did not hit the field perpendicularly. Since the plane struck at an angle, it's not surprising that high-mass items like the engine fan would be expelled. "Because the engines weigh somewhere around 1,000 pounds, they come off very early in the accident sequence and are basically thrown out of the impact crater, in the direction the plane was traveling," Feith says.

"It's not unusual for an engine to move or tumble across the ground," agrees Michael K. Hynes, an airline accident expert who investigated the crash of TWA Flight 800 out of New York City in 1996. "When you have very high velocities, 500 miles per hour or more, you are talking about 700 to 800 feet per second. For something to hit the ground with that kind of energy, it would only take a few seconds to bounce up and travel 300 yards."

This scenario of heavy items being propelled ahead of the wreckage is not unusual: On September 11 it also occurred when the landing gear and black box of Flight 77 were found deep inside the Pentagon, far from their original position in the aircraft.

Todd Curtis of AirSafe.com, a former Boeing safety inspector, helped investigate the 1995 crash of an AWACS E-3 radar plane in Alaska. In that crash, he says, the bulk of the plane was almost completely obliterated but "one of the engines had gone a quarter-mile away and was sitting unscathed in the woods."

# Indian Lake

CLAIM: "Residents and workers at businesses outside Shanksville, Somerset County, reported discovering clothing, books, papers and what appeared to be human remains," states a *Pittsburgh Post-Gazette* article dated September 13, 2001. "Others reported what appeared to be crash debris floating in Indian Lake, nearly six miles from the immediate crash scene." This raises questions for some conspiracy theorists. Commenting on reports that Indian Lake residents collected debris, www.thinkandask.com speculates: "On September 10, 2001, a strong cold front pushed through the area, and behind it—winds blew northerly. Since Flight 93 crashed west-southwest of Indian Lake, it was impossible for debris to fly perpendicular to wind direction. The plane had to have flown overhead. The FBI lied." The Web site www.theforbiddenknowledge.com concludes that the widespread debris proves the plane was breaking up prior to impact: "Without a doubt, Flight 93 was shot down."

FACT: Wallace Miller, Somerset County coroner, tells *Popular Mechanics* that no body parts were found in Indian Lake. Human remains were confined to a 70-acre area directly surrounding the crash site. Paper and tiny scraps of sheet metal, however, did land in the lake. "Very light debris will fly into the air, because of the concussion," says Matthew McCormick, who investigated the accident for the NTSB. Indian Lake is less than 1.5 miles southeast of the impact crater as the crow flies—not 6 miles, as indicated by online driving directions—easily within range of debris blasted skyward by the explosion from the crash.

How did the conspiracy Web site mistakenly believe the wind was blowing away from Indian Lake? First, the wind that day was northwesterly, at 9 to 12 miles per hour, which means it was blowing from the northwest—toward Indian Lake (see map 25). Second, the Web site reports Flight 93 crashed "west-southwest of Indian Lake," when it actually crashed northwest of the lake.

Nearly 1,500 rescue workers and investigators searched the area for 12 days, gathering evidence, including human remains. McCormick, now retired after 33 years with the NTSB, spent seven days at the site. He says, "From my investigation, there was no pre-impact stress to the airplane."

# AFTERWORD

## The Conspiracy Industry,
## by James B. Meigs
## Editor-In-Chief, *Popular Mechanics*

O n February 7, 2005, I became a member of the Bush/Halliburton/Zionist/CIA/New World Order/Illuminati conspiracy for global domination. It was on that day the March 2005 issue of *Popular Mechanics*, with its cover story debunking 9/11 conspiracy theories, hit newsstands. Within hours, the online community of 9/11 conspiracy buffs—which calls itself the "9/11 Truth Movement"—was aflame with wild fantasies about me and my staff, the magazine I edit, and the article we had published.

The Web site www.911research.wtc7.net, an organization that claims that questioning the "official" story of 9/11 is "an act of responsible citizenship," fired one of the first salvos: "Popular Mechanics Attacks Its 9/11 LIES Straw Man," read the headline of a piece by a leading conspiracy theorist named Jim Hoffman.

We had begun our plunge down the rabbit hole. Within hours, a post on www.portland.indymedia.org, which claims to be dedicated to "radical, accurate, and passionate tellings of truth," called me "James Meigs the Coward and Traitor." Not long afterward, another prominent conspiracy theorist produced an analysis that concluded that *Popular Mechanics* is a CIA front organization. Invective and threats soon clogged the comments section of our Web site and poured in by e-mail:

> I was amused at your attempts to prove the conspirator theorists wrong by your interviewing people who work for the government. Face it: The U.S. government planned this attack to further its own agenda in the Middle East.

> Rest assured, puppet boys . . . when the hammer comes down about the biggest crime ever perpetrated in the history of man—AND IT WILL—it will be VERY easy to identify the co-conspirators by their flimsy, awkwardly ignorant of reality magazine articles. Keep that in mind the next time you align yourself with evil scum.

> YOU HAVE DECLARD YOURSELF ENEMY OF AMERICANS AND FRIEND OF THE MOSSAD!

I shouldn't have been surprised. In researching the article we'd spent enough time studying the conspiracy movement to get a feel for its style: the tone of outraged patriotism, the apocalyptic rhetoric, the casual use of invective. A common refrain in conspiracy circles is the claim that "We're just asking questions." One would think that at least some quarters of the conspiracy movement might welcome a mainstream publication's serious, nonideological attempt to answer those questions. One would be wrong.

It was only a matter of time before the Nazis got dragged in. Christopher Bollyn, a prominent conspiracy theorist affiliated with the far-right American Free Press, weighed in a few weeks later with a piece titled "The Hidden Hand of the CIA, 911 And Popular Mechanics." The article begins with a brief history of Hitler's consolidation of power following the Reichstag fire in 1933. "Like Nazi Germany of 1933," Bollyn wrote, "American newsstands today carry a mainstream magazine dedicated to pushing the government's truth of 9/11 while viciously smearing independent researchers as extremists who peddle fantasies and make poisonous claims."

In a few short weeks, *Popular Mechanics* had gone from being a 100-year-old journal about science, engineering, car maintenance, and home improvement to being a pivotal player in a global conspiracy on a par with Nazi Germany.

Not all the responses were negative, of course. One visitor to our Web site, after plowing through dozens of angry comments, left a supportive post that included this astute observation:

> Some people are open to any possibility, and honestly examine all evidence in a rational manner to come to a conclusion, followed by a moral evaluation. Others start with a desire for a specific moral evaluation, and then work backwards assembling any fact that supports them, and dismissing any fact that does not.

Author Chip Berlet, who is an analyst for the liberal think tank Political Research Associates, employs the awkward but useful term "conspiracism" to describe this mindset. "Populist conspiracism sees secret plots by tiny cabals of evildoers as the major motor powering important historical events," he writes on the think tank's Web site. Berlet has spent more than two decades studying far-right and authoritarian movements in the United States. "Every major traumatic event in U.S. history generates a new round of speculation about conspiracies," he writes. "The attacks on 9/11/01 are no exception."

As the hate mail poured in and articles claiming to have debunked the magazine's analysis proliferated online, we soon learned to identify the key techniques that give conspiracy theorists their illusion of coherence.

# Marginalization of Opposing Views

The 9/11 Truth Movement invariably describes the mainstream account of 9/11 as the "government version" or "the official version." In fact, the generally accepted account of 9/11 is made up of a multitude of sources: thousands of newspaper, TV, and radio reports produced by journalists from all over the world; investigations conducted by independent organizations and institutions, including the American Society of Civil Engineers, Purdue University, Northwestern University, Columbia University, the National Fire Protection Association, and Underwriters Laboratories, Inc.; eyewitness testimony from literally thousands of people;

recordings and transcripts of phone calls, air traffic control transmissions, and other communications; thousands of photographs; thousands of feet of video footage; and, let's not forget the words of Osama bin Laden, who discussed the operation in detail on more than one occasion, including in an audio recording released in May 2006 that said: "I am responsible for assigning the roles of the 19 brothers to conduct these conquests . . ."

The mainstream view of 9/11 is, in other words, a vast consensus. By presenting it instead as the product of a small coterie of insiders, conspiracists are able to ignore facts they find inconvenient and demonize people with whom they disagree.

# Argument by Anomaly

In an article about the *Popular Mechanics* 9/11 report, *Scientific American* columnist Michael Shermer makes an important observation about the conspiracist method: "The mistaken belief that a handful of unexplained anomalies can undermine a well-established theory lies at the heart of all conspiratorial thinking (as well as creationism, Holocaust denial and the various crank theories of physics). All the 'evidence' for a 9/11 conspiracy falls under the rubric of this fallacy."

A successful scientific theory organizes masses of information into a coherent, well-tested narrative. When a theory has managed to explain the real world accurately enough for long enough, it becomes accepted as fact. Conspiracy theorists, Shermer points out, generally ignore the mass of evidence that supports the mainstream view and focus strictly on tiny anomalies. But, in a complex and messy world, the fact that there might be a few details we don't yet understand should not be surprising.

A good example is the conspiracist fascination with the collapse of 7 World Trade Center. Since the 47-story tower was not hit by an airplane, only by the debris of the North Tower, investigators weren't sure at first just how or why it collapsed hours after the attacks. A scientist (or for that matter, a journalist or historian) might see that gap in our knowledge as an opportunity for further research (see "WTC 7: Fire and Debris Damage," page 53). In the conspiracy world, however, even a hint of uncertainty is a chance to set a trap. If researchers can't "prove" exactly how the building fell, they say, then there is only one other possible conclusion: Someone blew it up.

# Slipshod Handling of Facts

There are hundreds of books—and hundreds of thousands of Web pages—devoted to 9/11 conspiracy theories, many bristling with footnotes, citations, and technical jargon. But despite the appearance of scholarly rigor, few of these documents handle factual material with enough care to pass muster at a high-school newspaper, much less at a scholarly journal. Some mistakes are mere sloppiness; others show deliberate disregard for the truth.

Journalism is never perfect. Early accounts of any major event are studded with minor errors and omissions. As

*Washington Post* publisher Philip Graham famously noted, "Journalism is the first draft of history." In future drafts, errors are corrected, so anyone honestly attempting to understand an event relies more heavily on later investigations. Conspiracy theorists tend to do just the opposite. For example, the conspiracy Web site www.total911.info includes the headline "Video: CNN reported no plane hit pentagon." The item includes a clip from the morning of the attack, in which reporter Jamie McIntyre says, "There's no evidence of a plane having crashed anywhere near the Pentagon."

Today, we know why very little wreckage was visible from McIntyre's vantage point: Flight 77 didn't crash *near* the Pentagon. It crashed *into* the Pentagon. Traveling at 780 feet per second, it struck with such force that virtually the entire aircraft and its contents continued into the building. Investigators recovered the shredded remnants of the plane, including the black box, and established exactly how Flight 77 struck the building. Through forensics they have identified all but five of the 64 passengers and crew and Pentagon fatalities. (All five hijackers were positively identified.) Though a few conspiracy theorists attempt to reckon with that vast accretion of evidence, many more prefer to turn back the clock to the earliest possible moment, when hard facts were at a minimum.

Some errors are so simple they are almost laughable. After the *Popular Mechanics* report was published, numerous critics wrote to object to our explanation of why NORAD was poorly prepared to intercept off-course commercial aircraft (see "Military Intercepts," page 22). Many pointed to the 1999 case of golfer Payne Stewart's private jet, which was intercepted and followed after losing pressurization and failing to respond to radio calls. "Within less than 20 minutes fighter planes were alongside Stewart's plane," one letter claimed. In fact, the widespread idea that a fighter was able to reach Stewart's aircraft within minutes is based on a convenient misreading of the flight records. According to the National Transportation Safety Board report on the incident, controllers lost contact with Stewart's jet at 9:30 a.m. eastern daylight time; the flight was intercepted at 9:52 a.m. *central daylight time*—that is, the intercept took an hour and 22 minutes, *not* 22 minutes. (Not surprisingly, such errors always seem to break in favor of the conspiracists' views and never the other way around.)

## Repetition

The Web site www.rense.com, which is edited by conspiracy-oriented radio talk-show host Jeff Rense, includes an article by Bollyn discussing the seismic data recorded by Columbia University's Lamont-Doherty Earth Observatory at the time the two towers fell. "These unexplained 'spikes' in the seismic data lend credence to the theory that massive explosions at the base of the towers caused the collapses," Bollyn concludes. This claim, which originally appeared in the American Free Press, was decisively debunked in the *Popular Mechanics* magazine article (and is addressed here in "Seismic Spikes" in Chapter 2, "The World Trade Center"). The truth on this issue isn't hard to find: Lamont-Doherty's research is available to the public. Nonetheless, this claim from Bollyn's piece is repeated verbatim on more than 50 conspiracy sites today.

In the early days of the Internet, some commentators worried that material posted online would be ephemeral. In fact, the opposite is true. On the Internet, errors can last forever—repeated, cross-referenced, and passed from site to site in an endless daisy chain. The essentially nonchronological nature of the Internet contributes to this phenomenon. Many postings don't have dates, so it is difficult for readers to see what information has been disproven or superseded. Mainstream journalism makes at least an attempt to correct mistakes and prevent them from being repeated in later stories. The conspiracy movement prefers a see-what-sticks approach: Throw everything against the wall, and keep throwing.

# Circular Reasoning

In archaeology, researchers are often reminded that the absence of evidence is not evidence of absence. In the world of 9/11 denial, even the tiniest gaps in the evidence record are seen as proof that the mainstream view is incorrect. Case in point: the widespread claim that the government was hiding incriminating evidence because it refused to release video footage from security cameras outside the Pentagon. The footage had been entered into evidence at the trial of Al Qaeda conspirator Zacarias Moussaoui, who pleaded guilty in May 2006. Later that month the government released the material in response to a Freedom of Information request by the conservative watchdog organization Judicial Watch. The footage from two of those cameras, however, didn't show the cruise missile or small aircraft predicted by author Thierry Meyssan and others. Nor did it show a Boeing 757 streaking toward impact. In fact, the security cameras in question recorded data at the glacial rate of one frame per second. The odds of picking up a clear image of a jet moving at 780 feet per second were slim indeed. But that didn't stop an online commentator from concluding: "There's no plane at the Pentagon at 9/11, plain and simple."

But among 9/11 theorists, the *presence* of evidence supporting the mainstream view is also taken as proof of conspiracy. One forum posting that has multiplied across the Internet includes a long list of the physical evidence linking the 19 hijackers to the crime: the rental car left behind at Boston's Logan airport, Mohamed Atta's suitcase, passports recovered at the crash sites, and so on. "HOW CONVENIENT!" the author notes after each citation. In the heads-I-win-tails-you-lose logic of conspiracism, there is no piece of information that cannot be incorporated into one's pet theory. Like doctrinaire Marxists or certain religious extremists, conspiracists enjoy a worldview that is immune to refutation.

Jim Hoffman sums up this worldview nicely in one of his pieces attacking the original *Popular Mechanics* investigation of conspiracy theories. "[The article] purports to debunk conspiracy theorists' physical-evidence-based claims without even acknowledging that there are other grounds on which to question the official story," he writes. "Indeed many 9/11 researchers don't even address the physical evidence, preferring instead to focus on who had the means, motive, and opportunity to carry out the attack." This is a stunning burst of honesty: Since we've already decided who's to blame, Hoffman is saying, evidence is optional.

# Demonization

The 9/11 conspiracy theorists have an eternal problem: In every field where they make claims, the leading experts disagree with them. The only solution is to attack these authorities early and often.

Van Romero, an explosives expert from New Mexico who was quoted in the *Albuquerque Journal* on September 11, 2001, as saying that it looked like explosives brought down the World Trade Center towers, saw this firsthand. Eleven days later, the *Journal* ran a follow-up story stating his opinion that "fire is what caused the buildings to fail." Predictably, conspiracists view that clarification as proof that somebody "got to" Romero. "Directly or indirectly, pressure was brought to bear, forcing Romero to retract his original statement," claimed www.emperors-clothes.com.

It is in the nature of conspiracy theories that they must constantly expand as they try to absorb and neutralize conflicting information. In the immediate aftermath of the attacks, a conspiracy theorist might have imagined a compact plot involving a corrupt White House and a few renegade military officers. But as the months went by, committees were organized by Congress, the Federal Emergency Management Agency, the National Institute of Standards and Technology, the American Society of Civil Engineers, and others. News organizations conducted detailed investigations. Reports and studies piled up, none of them helpful to the conspiracist viewpoint. For conspiracy theorists there was only one answer: All of these people must be in on the plot, too.

One of the chilling things about 9/11 denial is how blithely its adherents are able to accuse their fellow citizens of complicity in evil. They think nothing of suggesting that Romero would keep silent about an enormous crime, that hundreds of researchers involved in 9/11 investigations were participants in a cover-up, or that journalists from *Popular Mechanics*, *The Nation*, the *New York Times* and hundreds of other publications would willingly hide such a plot. Many critics of *Popular Mechanics* complained that some of the sources we quoted work for the U.S. government. The assumption—explicitly stated by many—was that *anyone* connected with the government should be seen as implicated. Point of reference: Not including the U.S. Post Office, the federal government has more than 2 million employees.

# Guilt by Association

Soon after the *Popular Mechanics* report appeared, conspiracy buffs began parsing the names of the various researchers who contributed to the article, noting the odd coincidence that Benjamin Chertoff, then the head of the magazine's research department, has the same last name as the then newly appointed head of the Department of Homeland Security, Michael Chertoff. In a rare instance of reportorial initiative (most 9/11 "Internet researchers" rarely venture beyond Google), Christopher Bollyn phoned Ben's mother, who volunteered that, yes, she thinks Michael Chertoff might be a distant cousin. "Chertoff's Cousin Penned *Popular Mechanics* 9/11 Hit Piece," read the headline on Bollyn's next American

Free Press story. "This is exactly the kind of 'journalism' one would expect to find in a dictatorship like that of Saddam Hussein's Iraq," he concluded. Later, a headline was added to his article: "Ben Chertoff: Propagandist & Illuminati Disinformation Tool."

As often happens in the world of conspiracy theories, a grain of truth—it's possible that Ben and Michael Chertoff are distantly related—was built into a towering dune. In fact, Ben and Michael Chertoff have never spoken. And no one at *Popular Mechanics* had any contact with Michael Chertoff's office while preparing the article. Moreover, Ben was one of many researchers on the story, not the author. (Then, of course, there's the question of *why* Ben—and his colleagues—would be eager to get involved with one of the greatest crimes in history.) But in the world of 9/11 conspiracy theories, coincidence is proof of collaboration.

# The Paranoid Style

The conspiracist worldview is reflected in our culture of Oliver Stone movies, *X-Files* episodes, and *The Da Vinci Code*. But its roots go deeper. In 1964, historian Richard Hofstadter published his famous essay, "The Paranoid Style in American Politics," in *Harper's* magazine. His topic was America's long history of grassroots movements organized to oppose various perceived conspiracies. While the targets of suspicion might vary—Masons, Catholics, "international bankers"—the tone of these movements, what Hofstadter calls their paranoid style, does not. He uses the term *paranoid* not in the clinical sense, he says, but because no other word captures "the sense of heated exaggeration, suspiciousness, and conspiratorial fantasy" that is the hallmark of this worldview.

He quotes a classic example of conspiracist rhetoric:

> How can we account for our present situation unless we believe that men high in this government are concerting to deliver us to disaster? This must be the product of a great conspiracy on a scale so immense as to dwarf any previous such venture in the history of man. . . . What can be made of this unbroken series of decisions and acts contributing to the strategy of defeat? They cannot be attributed to incompetence. . . .

Compare that passage to this more recent expression of the same sentiment:

> In fact, conspiracy is very plausible. People who control a grossly disproportionate share of the world's wealth will take measures to consolidate their position. They will destabilize the public by inciting a series of wars and other mind-boggling hoaxes. . . . The government-inspired 9-11 atrocity proves Bush and his accomplices are criminals, traitors and impostors. . . .

The first quotation is from Senator Joe McCarthy, speaking in 1951 about the vast army of Communists he claimed had infiltrated the U.S. government. The second is from the Web site www.rense.com. Leaving aside references to Bush and 9/11, the two passages are essentially interchangeable.

Both share the view that some disaster has befallen the country that mere bungling on the part of our top officials cannot explain. Grander forces must be at work.

Hofstadter's main focus was the rise of the paranoid style among far-right political groups such as McCarthy's supporters and the John Birch Society, an ultra-conservative anticommunist organization. At their most extreme, some members of this movement believed that Presidents Truman and Eisenhower were Communist agents. Hofstadter would have recognized today's 9/11 conspiracy proponents as the earlier theorists' ideological soul mates. Deep down, he argues, conspiracists revel in their self-defined status as society's Cassandras: "As a member of the avant-garde who is capable of perceiving the conspiracy before it is fully obvious to an as yet unaroused public, the paranoid is a militant leader," he wrote. "He is always manning the barricades of civilization. He constantly lives at a turning point."

Those barricades are getting crowded. The documentary *Loose Change*, a messy grab bag of thinly sourced conspiracy claims, became a campus and Internet sensation in 2005. Conspiracy groups recently began hosting conventions where hundreds of like-minded "skeptics" gather to compare notes. And conspiracy literature has become commonplace at antiwar marches and other political events. Most of those embracing the conspiracist mindset probably believe they are espousing a left-wing view. But dig deep enough in the "9/11 Truth Movement" and you come to a place where left and right collide.

The movie *Loose Change*, for example, frequently cites the American Free Press (AFP) as a source. According to the watchdog group, Center for Media and Democracy, AFP has its roots in the now defunct Liberty Lobby, a group associated with racism, anti-Semitism, and Holocaust denial. (Its founder, Willis Carto, was once described as "America's most successful professional anti-Semite and racist.") The award-winning liberal news site www.alternet.org says "the ability of the right-wing media apparatus to dominate public discourse is at the expense of liberal and progressive values." The site's mission statement concludes: "This is what we are fighting against." Yet, when the Web site offers a roundup of conspiracy theories, it lists www.rense.com as a source. Among the thousands of articles included on the Rense site are a disturbing number dealing with the influence of Israel on world events and doubts about the reality of the Holocaust. (In a disclaimer, Rense notes that inclusion of an article on his site does not constitute endorsement.) In one piece, titled "Auschwitz—Myths & Facts," the reader is informed that "Auschwitz was not an extermination center and that the story of mass killings in 'gas chambers' is a myth."

Strange bedfellows, indeed. In truth, the worldviews of far-left- and far-right-wing conspiracists differ little. Both think that vast, malevolent forces have hijacked American democracy. And both believe that the press, our elected officials, and the American people—or "sheeple," as today's conspiracists like to call them—are too timid and ignorant to speak up. As Hofstadter shows, such sentiments have been around since the early days of the republic. But 9/11 gave modern conspiracists a huge historical tragedy to examine through their ideological lenses and to recast with their favorite villains.

The American public has every right to demand answers and all too many reasons to lack confidence in the government. Sadly, in such a climate, the fantasies of 9/11 conspiracists provide a seductive alternative to facing the hard facts and difficult choices of our time.

New York City
June 2006

## APPENDIX A

# EXPERTS
# CONSULTED

The reporting team consulted more than 300 experts and organizations in its investigation into 9/11 conspiracy theories. The following were particularly helpful.

### AIR CRASH ANALYSIS

BILL CROWLEY, special agent, FBI

RON DOKELL, president, Demolition Consultants

GREG FEITH, crash investigator and former senior investigator for the National Transportation Safety Board (NTSB)

RICHARD GAZARIK, staff writer, *Pittsburgh Tribune-Review*

YATES GLADWELL, pilot, VF Corporation

BILL HOPPER, communications manager, Pentagon Renovation and Construction Program

JERRY HOUSENGA, technical product specialist, Bosch Security Systems

MICHAEL K. HYNES, Ed.D., ATP, CFI, A&P/IA president, Hynes Aviation Services

CHERYL IRWIN, public affairs, Office of the Secretary of Defense

EDWARD JACOBY JR., director, New York State Emergency Management Office (Ret.) Johnstown-Cambria County Airport Authority

CINDI LASH, staff writer, *Pittsburgh Post-Gazette*

MATTHEW MCCORMICK, manager, Survival Factors Division, NTSB (Ret.)

WALLACE MILLER, coroner, Somerset County, PA

Robert Nagan, meteorological technician, Climate Services Branch, National Climatic Data Center

Dave Newell, director, aviation and travel, VF Corporation

James O'Toole, politics editor, *Pittsburgh Post-Gazette*

Jeff Pillets, senior writer, *The Record*, Hackensack, N.J.

Jeff Reinbold, director, Flight 93 National Memorial, National Park Service

Dennis Roddy, staff writer, *Pittsburgh Post-Gazette*

Master Sgt. David E. Somdahl, public affairs officer, 119th Wing, North Dakota Air National Guard

Mark Stahl, photographer; eyewitness, United Airlines Flight 93 crash scene

Mike Walter, television anchor, WUSA

## AIR DEFENSE

Lt. Col. Skip Aldous (Ret.), squadron commander, U.S. Air Force

Tech. Sgt. Laura Bosco, public affairs officer, Tyndall Air Force Base

Laura Brown, spokeswoman, Federal Aviation Administration (FAA)

Todd Curtis, Ph.D., founder, Airsafe.com; president, Airsafe.com Foundation

Michael Friel, director, Border Security Media Division, U.S. Customs and Border Protection

Keith Halloway, public affairs officer, NTSB

Ted Lopatkiewicz, director, public affairs, NTSB

Maj. Douglas Martin, former public affairs officer, North American Aerospace Defense Command (NORAD)

Lt. Herbert McConnell, public affairs officer, Andrews Air Force Base

Staff Sgt. Sean McEntee, 113th Wing of the District of Columbia National Guard

Crystal M. Oliver, public affairs, U.S. Army

Michael Perini, public affairs officer, NORAD

John Pike, director, GlobalSecurity.org

Hank Price, spokesman, FAA

Gen. Hugh Shelton (Ret.), chairman, Joint Chiefs of Staff

Bill Shumann, spokesman, FAA

Louis Walsh, public affairs officer, Eglin AFB

Chris Yates, aviation security editor, analyst, *Jane's Defence Weekly*

## AVIATION

Fred E. C. Culick, Ph.D., S.B., S.M., professor of aeronautics, California Institute of Technology

Robert Everdeen, public affairs, Northrop Grumman

Paul Guckian, vice president of engineering, Qualcomm

RICK KEMPER, director of wireless technology, CTIA—The Wireless Association

BRIAN MARSH, flight instructor, Airline Transportation Professionals Flight School

CLINT OSTER, professor of public and environmental affairs, Indiana University

CAPT. BILL SCOTT (Ret. USAF), Rocky Mountain bureau chief, *Aviation Week*

MAJ. DARREN STEELE, public affairs, NORAD

BILL UHER, News Media Office, NASA Langley Research Center

COL. ED WALBY (Ret. USAF), director, business development, HALE Systems Enterprise, Unmanned Systems, Northrop Grumman

TIM WAGNER, spokesman, American Airlines

## IMAGE ANALYSIS

WILLIAM F. BAKER, partner, Skidmore, Owings and Merrill

MARC BIRNBACH, videographer, president, Avenue Z Productions

W. GENE CORLEY, Ph.D., P.E., S.E., senior vice president, CTL Group

BILL DALY, senior vice president, Control Risks Group

STEVE DOUGLASS, image analysis consultant, *Aviation Week*

THOMAS R. EDWARDS, Ph.D., founder, TREC

RONALD GREELEY, Ph.D., professor of geology, Arizona State University

ROB HOWARD, freelance photographer; WTC eyewitness

ROBERT L. PARKER, Ph.D., professor of geophysics, University of California, San Diego

## STRUCTURAL ENGINEERING/BUILDING COLLAPSE

FARID ALFAWAKHIRI, Ph.D., senior engineer, American Iron and Steel Institute

JONATHAN BARNETT, professor of fire protection engineering, Worcester Polytechnic Institute

ZDENEK BAZANT, Ph.D., professor of civil engineering, Northwestern University

DAVID BIGGS, P.E., structural engineer, Ryan-Biggs Associates

BRENT BLANCHARD, operations manager, Protec Documentation Services Inc.

LOUIE CACCHIOLI, firefighter, Fire Department of New York City (FDNY) (Ret.)

JOSEPH CARSKY, chief engineer, Tully Construction

ROBERT CLARKE, structural engineer, Controlled Demolitions Group Ltd.

GLENN CORBETT, technical editor, *Fire Engineering*

VINCENT DUNN, deputy fire chief (Ret.), FDNY; author, *The Collapse of Burning Buildings: A Guide to Fireground Safety*

JOHN FISHER, Ph.D., professor of civil engineering, Lehigh University

RICHARD FRUEHAN, professor of metallurgical engineering, Carnegie Mellon University

KEN HAYS, executive vice president, Masonry Arts

CHRISTOPH HOFFMANN, Ph.D., professor of computer science, Purdue University

ALLYN E. KILSHEIMER, P.E., CEO, KCE Structural Engineers PC

WON-YOUNG KIM, Ph.D., seismologist, Lamont-Doherty Earth Observatory, Columbia University

WILLIAM KOPLITZ, photo desk manager, FEMA

JOHN LABRIOLA, freelance photographer; WTC survivor

ARTHUR LERNER-LAM, Ph.D., seismologist; director, Earth Institute, Center for Hazards and Risk Research, Columbia University

MATTHYS LEVY, structural engineer and principal, Weidlinger Associates; coauthor of *Why Buildings Fall Down*

MARK LOIZEAUX, co-owner, Controlled Demolition, Inc.

STACEY LOIZEAUX, project manager, Controlled Demolition, Inc.

JON MAGNUSSON, structural engineer, chairman and CEO of Magnusson Klemencic Associates

PAUL MLAKAR, senior research scientist, U.S. Army Engineer Research and Development Center; team leader, *The Pentagon Building Performance Report*

ALAN PENSE, professor emeritus of metallurgical engineering, Lehigh University

JAMES QUINTIERE, Ph.D., professor of engineering, University of Maryland

STEVE RISKUS, freelance photographer; eyewitness, Pentagon crash

VAN ROMERO, Ph.D., vice president, New Mexico Institute of Mining and Technology

CHRISTINE SHAFFER, spokesperson, Viracon

METE SOZEN, Ph.D., professor of structural engineering, Purdue University

SHYAM SUNDER, Sc.D., acting deputy director, lead investigator, Building and Fire Research Laboratory, National Institute of Standards and Technology (NIST)

ERIC TERRILL, director, Coastal Observing Research and Development Center at the Scripps Institution of Oceanography

MARY TOBIN, media relations, Earth Institute, Columbia University

FORMAN WILLIAMS, Ph.D., professor of engineering, physics, combustion, University of California, San Diego

# WORLD TRADE CENTER REPORT

The following material is abridged from the *Final Report of the National Construction Safety Team on the Collapses of the World Trade Center*, which was prepared for the National Institute of Standards and Technology (NIST), a nonregulatory agency of the U.S. Department of Commerce's Technology Administration. More than 200 staffers and NIST contractors conducted interviews with more than 1,000 people who were on the scene or were involved with the design, construction, and maintenance of the WTC; analyzed 236 pieces of steel recovered from the site; performed laboratory tests that measured material properties; and performed computer simulations of the sequence of events from the impact of the aircraft to the initiation of collapse for each tower. In addition, the NIST staff accumulated 7,000 segments of video footage of the event totaling more than 150 hours, as well as nearly 7,000 photographs from 185 photographers on the scene that day.

The report, which took three years to produce and cost $24 million, was released in September 2005. To read the complete document, which includes 43 separate reports totaling some 10,000 pages, go to http://wtc.nist.gov/pubs.

# Executive Summary

## E.3 SUMMARY OF FINDINGS

Objective 1: Determine why and how WTC 1 and WTC 2 collapsed following the initial impacts of the aircraft.

- The two aircraft hit the towers at high speed and did considerable damage to principal structural components: core columns, floors, and perimeter columns. However, the towers withstood the impacts and would have remained standing were it not for the dislodged insulation (fireproofing) and the subsequent multifloor fires. The robustness of the perimeter frame-tube system and the large size of the buildings helped the towers withstand the impact. The structural system redistributed loads without collapsing in places of aircraft impact, avoiding larger scale damage upon impact. The hat truss, a feature atop each tower which was intended to support a television antenna, prevented earlier collapse of the building core. In each tower, a different combination of impact damage and heat-weakened structural components contributed to the abrupt structural collapse.

- In WTC 1, the fires weakened the core columns and caused the floors on the south side of the building to sag. The floors pulled the heated south perimeter columns inward, reducing their capacity to support the building above. Their neighboring columns quickly became overloaded as columns on the south wall buckled. The top section of the building tilted to the south and began its descent. The time from aircraft impact to collapse initiation was largely determined by how long it took for the fires to weaken the building's core and to reach the south side of the building and weaken the perimeter columns and floors.

- In WTC 2, the core was damaged severely at the southeast corner and was restrained by the east and south walls via the hat truss and the floors. The steady burning fires on the east side of the building caused the floors there to sag. The floors pulled the heated east perimeter columns inward, reducing their capacity to support the building above. Their neighboring columns quickly became overloaded as columns on the east wall buckled. The top section of the building tilted to the east and to the south and began its descent. The time from aircraft impact to collapse initiation was largely determined by the time for the fires to weaken the perimeter columns and floor assemblies on the east and the south sides of the building. WTC 2 collapsed more quickly than WTC 1 because there was more aircraft damage to the building core and there were early and persistent fires on the east side of the building, where the aircraft had extensively dislodged insulation from the structural steel.

- The WTC towers likely would not have collapsed under the combined effects of aircraft impact damage and the extensive, multifloor fires if the thermal insulation had not been widely dislodged or had been only minimally dislodged by aircraft impact.

# Chapter 1: New York's World Trade Center

## 1.2 THE WORLD TRADE CENTER COMPLEX

### The Structures

Each of the tenant floors of the towers was intended to offer a large expanse of workspace, virtually uninterrupted by columns or walls. This called for an innovative structural design, lightweight to minimize the total mass of 110 stories, yet strong enough to support the huge building with all its furnishings and people. Structural engineers refer to the building weight as the *dead load*; the people and furnishings are called the *live load*. Collectively, these are referred to as *gravity loads*. The buildings would also need to resist *lateral loads* and excessive swaying, principally from the hurricane-force winds that periodically strike the eastern seaboard of the United States. An additional load, stated by The Port Authority [of New York and New Jersey, the owner of the WTC] to have been considered in the design of the towers, was the impact of a Boeing 707, the largest commercial airliner when the towers were designed, hitting the building at its full speed of 600 mph. Skilling and his team [engineer John Skilling, a partner in the firm Worthington, Skilling, Helle and Jackson] rose to the challenge of providing the required load capacity within Yamasaki's [WTC architect Minoru Yamaski] design concept. They incorporated an innovative framed-tube concept for the structural system. The columns supporting the building were located both along the external faces and within the core. The core also contained the elevators, stairwells, and utility shafts. The dense array of columns along the building perimeter was to resist the lateral load due to hurricane-force winds, while also sharing the gravity loads about equally

with the core columns. The floor system was to provide stiffness and stability to the framed-tube system in addition to supporting the floor loads.
Extensive and detailed studies were conducted in wind tunnels, instead
of relying on specific, prescriptive building code requirements, to estimate
the wind loads used in the design of these buildings. This approach took
advantage of the allowance by some state and local building codes for
alternative designs and construction if evidence were presented that
ensured equivalent performance.

There were four major structural subsystems in the towers, referred to
as the exterior wall, the core, the floor system, and the hat truss. The first,
the exterior structural subsystem, was a vertical square tube that consisted
of 236 narrow columns, 59 on each face from the 10th floor to the 107th
floor. There were also columns on alternate stories at each of the beveled
corners, but these carried none of the gravity loads. (There were fewer,
wider-spaced columns below the 7th floor to accommodate doorways.)

Each column was fabricated by welding four steel plates to form a tall
box, nominally 14 in. on a side. The space between the steel columns was
26 in., with a narrower, framed plate glass window in each gap. Adjacent
columns were connected at each floor by steel spandrel plates, 52 in. high.
The upper parts of the buildings had less wind load and building mass to
support. Thus, on higher floors, the thickness of the steel plates making up
the columns decreased, becoming as thin as ¼ in. near the top. There were
10 grades of steel used for the columns and spandrels, with yield strengths
ranging from 36 ksi to 100 ksi [kips per square inch—a measurement of
stress intensity]. The grade of steel used in each location was dictated by the
calculated stresses due to the gravity and wind loads.

All the exterior columns and spandrels were prefabricated into welded
panels, three stories tall and three columns wide. The panels, each numbered to identify its location in the tower, were then bolted to adjacent units
to form the walls. The use of identically shaped prefabricated elements was
itself an innovation that enabled rapid construction. The high degree of
modularization and prefabrication used in the construction of these buildings and the identification, tracking, and logistics necessary to ensure that
each piece was positioned correctly was unprecedented.

A second structural subsystem was located in a central service area, or
core, approximately 135 ft by 87 ft, that extended virtually the full height
of the building. The long axis of the core in WTC 1 was oriented in the
east-west direction, while the long axis of the core in WTC 2 was oriented
in the north-south direction. The 47 columns in this rectangular space were
fabricated using primarily 36 ksi and 42 ksi steels and also decreased in
size at the higher stories. The four massive corner columns bore nearly

one-fifth of the total gravity load on the core columns. The core columns were interconnected by a grid of conventional steel beams to support the core floors.

The third major structural subsystem was the floors in the tenant spaces. These floors supported their own weight, along with live loads, provided lateral stability to the exterior walls, and distributed wind loads among the exterior walls. The floor construction was an innovation for a tall building. Each tenant floor consisted of 4 in. thick, lightweight cast-in-place concrete on a fluted steel deck, but that is where "ordinary" ended. Supporting the slab was a grid of lightweight steel bar trusses. The top bends (or "knuckles") of the main truss webs extended 3 in. above the top chord and were embedded into the concrete floor slab. This concrete and steel assembly thus functioned as a composite unit—that is, the concrete slab acted integrally with the steel trusses to carry bending loads. The primary truss pairs were either 60 ft or 35 ft long and were spaced at 6 ft 8 in. intervals. There were perpendicular bridging trusses every 13 ft 4 in. The floor trusses and fluted metal deck were prefabricated in panels that were typically 20 ft wide and that were hoisted into position in a fashion similar to the exterior wall panels.

The bottom chords were connected to the spandrel plates by devices that were called viscoelastic dampers. Experiments on motion perception, conducted with human subjects, had shown a high potential for occupant discomfort when the building swayed in a strong wind. When the tower was buffeted by strong winds, these dampers absorbed energy, reducing the sway and the vibration expected from a building that tall. The use of such vibration damping devices in buildings was an innovation at that time.

The fourth major structural subsystem was located from the 107th floor to the roof of each tower. It was a set of steel braces, collectively referred to as the "hat truss." Its primary purpose had been to support a tall antenna atop each tower, although only WTC 1 had one installed. The hat truss provided additional connections among the core columns and between the core and perimeter columns, providing additional means for load redistribution.

# Chapter 2: The Account of World Trade Center 1

## 2.2 THE AIRCRAFT

The Boeing 767-200ER was a twin-engine, wide-body aircraft, 159 ft 2 in. long, with a wingspan of 156 ft 1 in. Empty, it weighed 183,500 lb.

It could carry 181 passengers in its three-class seating configuration and 23,980 gal (158,200 lb) of jet fuel as it covered its maximum cruising range of 6,600 miles. The maximum total weight the plane could carry was specified at 395,000 lb; the typical cruising speed was 530 mph.

On that day, AA Flight 11 was much lighter. Bound from Boston for Los Angeles, some 3,000 miles away, it carried only about half the full load of jet fuel. When it hit the North Tower, it likely contained about 10,000 gal (66,000 lb), evenly distributed between the right and left wing tanks. Because of the tight maneuvers as the plane approached the tower, the baffles in both tanks had directed the fuel toward the inboard side of each wing. The passenger cabin was more than half empty. The cargo bay, carrying less than a full load of luggage, contained five tons of luggage, mail, electronic equipment, and food. The total weight of the aircraft was estimated to be 283,600 lb.

## 2.3 THE IMMEDIATE DAMAGE

The aircraft flew almost straight toward the North Tower, banked approximately 25 degrees to the left (i.e., the right wing elevated relative to the left wing) and descended at an angle of about 10 degrees at impact. Moving at about 440 mph, the nose hit the exterior of the tower at the 96th floor. The aircraft cut a gash that was over half the width of the building and extended from the 93rd floor to the 99th floor. All but the lowest of these floors were occupied by Marsh & McLennan, a worldwide insurance company, which also occupied the 100th floor. Marsh & McLennan shared the 93rd floor with Fred Alger Management, an investment portfolio management company. There was relatively little impact damage to the 93rd floor, hit only by the outboard 10 ft of the left wing. Containing no jet fuel, the wing tip was shredded by the perimeter columns. The light debris did minimal damage to the columns or to the thermal insulation on the trusses of the composite floor system supporting the 94th floor. The trusses supporting the 94th floor were impacted by flying debris on the 93rd floor.

The 94th floor was more severely damaged. The midsection of the left wing, laden with jet fuel, and the left engine cut through the building facade, severing 17 of the perimeter columns and heavily damaging four more. The pieces of the aircraft continued inward, severing and heavily damaging core columns. The insulation applied to the floor trusses above and the columns was scraped off by shrapnel-like aircraft debris and building wall fragments over a wedge almost 100 ft wide at the north face of the tower and 50 ft wide at the south end of the building core. The reader should bear in mind that the described damage to the building exterior comes from eyewitness and photographic evidence. The described damage to the aircraft and the building interior was deemed most likely from the computer simulations and analysis carried out under the investigation.

The 767-200ER aircraft had two fuel tanks that extended through most of the interior of the wings and a center tank between the wings in the bottom of the fuselage. A full fuel load would have filled all three tanks. The aircraft did the most damage to the 95th and 96th floors. The fuel-heavy inner left wing hit the 95th floor slab, breaking it over the full 60 ft depth of tenant space and another 20 ft into the building core. The fuselage was centered on the 96th floor slab and filled the 95th and 96th floors top to bottom. The severity of the impact was clear. A wheel from the left wing landing gear flew through multiple partitions, through the core of the building, and became embedded in one of the exterior column panels on the south side of the tower. The impact severed the bolts connecting the panel to its neighbors, and the panel and tire landed on Cedar Street, some 700 ft to the south. A second wheel landed 700 ft farther south. Within the two floors, 15 to 18 perimeter columns and five to six core columns were severed, and an additional one to three core columns were heavily damaged. A 40 ft width of the 96th floor slab was broken 80 ft into the building. The insulation was knocked off nearly all the core columns and over a 40 ft width of floor trusses from the south end of the core to the south face of the tower.

The right wing of the aircraft was fragmented by the perimeter columns on the 97th floor. In the process, 12 of those columns were severed. The debris cut a path through the west and center array of trusses and core columns, stripping the insulation over a 90 ft wide path. The insulation was stripped from a 50 ft wide path on the south side of the floor space. On the 98th and 99th floors, the outboard 30 ft of the starboard wing was sliced by the perimeter columns, of which five were severed. The debris cut a shallow path through the west and center array of trusses, damaging the insulation up to the north wall of the building core.

This devastation took 0.7 seconds. The structural and insulation damage was considerable and was estimated to be:

- 35 exterior columns severed, 2 heavily damaged.
- 6 core columns severed, 3 heavily damaged.
- 43 of 47 core columns stripped of insulation on one or more floors.
- Insulation stripped from trusses covering 60,000 square feet of floor area.

*Even with all this damage, the building still stood.* The acceleration from the impact had been so severe that people even on lower floors were knocked down and furniture was thrown about. Some survivors reported fallen ceiling tiles throughout the building, all the way down to the Concourse Level. The pipes that fed the automatic fire sprinkler system were severed. At least 166 windows were broken. Damage to interior walls was reported from the lobby to the 92nd floor. However, the building was designed with reserve capacity: It could support significantly more load than the weight of the structure and its people and contents. The building redistributed the load from the severed perimeter columns, mainly to their neighboring columns. The undamaged core columns assumed the remaining load, as well as the load from their damaged neighbors. WTC 1 still stood, and would have continued to do so, if not for the fires that followed.

## 2.4 THE JET FUEL

To the wings of the 767-200ER, the perimeter columns acted like knife blades, slashing the aluminum fuel tanks and atomizing much of the 10,000 gal of jet fuel liquid into a spray of fuel droplets. Atomized jet fuel is highly flammable (similar to kerosene), so both the hot debris and the numerous pieces of electrical and electronic gear in the offices were more than sufficient as ignition sources. A surge of combusting fuel rapidly filled the floors, mixing with dust from the pulverized walls and floor slabs. The pressure created by the heated gases forced the ignited mist out the entrance gash and blown-out windows on the east and south sides of the tower. The resulting fireballs could be seen for miles, precipitating many 9-1-1 calls.

Less than 15 percent of the jet fuel burned in the spray cloud inside the building. A roughly comparable amount was consumed in the fireballs outside the building. Thus, well over half of the jet fuel remained in the building, unburned in the initial fires. Some splashed onto the office furnishings and combustibles from the aircraft that lodged on the impacted floors, there to ignite (immediately or later) the fires that would continue to burn for the remaining life of the building. Some of the burning fuel shot up and down the elevator shafts, blowing out doors and walls on other floors all the way down to the basement. Flash fires in the lobby blew out many of the plate glass windows. Fortunately, there were not enough combustibles near the elevators for major fires to start on the lower floors.

## 2.7 9:03 A.M. TO 9:57 A.M. EDT

A fire needs a continuing supply of both gaseous fuel and oxygen if it is to keep burning, and the initially burning combustibles in WTC 1 were being consumed. The additional fuel came from the office furnishings next to those that were reaching the end of their burning life. The thermal radiation from the flames and from the hot gases heated the nearby combustibles, creating flammable vapors. These vapors needed a source of nearby air to continue the burning. The same flames and hot ceiling layer gases heated the windows and window frames in the vicinity. The hot gases pushed on the weakened aluminum frames, sending some windows outward to fall to the plaza below. Other windows were sucked into the building. The fires now had both new fuel and fresh air.

And so the fires continued to spread, likely aided by as-yet unburned jet fuel that had soaked into some of the furnishings and flooring. The coating of (non-combustible) gypsum and concrete fragments slowed the burning rate by as much as half, but could not halt the fire from spreading. The overall movement of the fires was toward the south side of the tower. By 9:15 a.m., the fires on the 97th floor had intensified and filled most of the floor. Large fires had erupted on the east sides of the 92nd and 96th floors. Seventy-five minutes after the impact, approaching 10:00 a.m., the fire on the 97th floor had begun to burn itself out, but the fire on the 94th floor had intensified and filled much of the north half of the floor. Starting about 9:30 a.m., there were vigorous fires on nearly the full perimeter of the 98th floor. There was still almost no burning on the 99th floor or above.

The hot smoke from the fires now filled nearly all the upper part of the tenant space on the impact floors. Aside from isolated areas, perhaps protected by surviving gypsum walls, the cooler parts of this upper layer were at about 500 °C [932 °F], and in the vicinity of the active fires, the upper layer air temperatures reached 1,000 °C [1,832 °F]. The aircraft fragments had broken through the core walls on the 94th through the 97th floors, and temperatures in the upper layers there were similar to those in the tenant spaces.

The perimeter columns, floors, and core columns were immersed in these hot gases and began to weaken. Where the insulation was dislodged, the temperature of the steel rose rapidly, in contrast to steel members where insulation was intact. The heaviest core columns with damaged insulation heated slowly, as the absorbed heat was dissipated through their massive cross sections. The temperatures of the lighter columns and the floor slabs rose more quickly, and those of the stripped trusses even more so.

As a steel column is heated, its ability to support gravity loads and resist lateral loads decreases. At temperatures of about 300 °C [572 °F], steel loses about 20 percent of its yield strength. Under modest loads, steel is *elastic*—that is, it can compress, or shorten, but will recover when loads are removed. As the load increases, the steel becomes *plastic*, and the shortening is unrecoverable. At still higher loads, the column buckles. At temperatures above 500 °C, the steel weakens, the loss of strength and stiffness become significant, and the column's ability to carry its share of the building loads decreases. It shortens due to a combination of plastic deformation and an additional, time-dependent deformation called *creep* that can increase column shortening and hasten buckling.

At this point, the core of WTC 1 could be imagined to be in three sections. There was a bottom section below the impact floors that could be thought of as a strong, rigid box, structurally undamaged and at almost normal temperature. There was a top section above the impact and fire floors that was also a heavy, rigid box. In the middle was the third section, partially damaged by the aircraft and weakened by heat from the fires. The core of the top section tried to move downward, but was held up by the hat truss. The hat truss, in turn, redistributed the load to the perimeter columns.

(Structural steels do not need to melt to lose strength. Their melting points are about 1,600 °C [2,912 °F], well above the 1,100 °C [2012 °F] typical peak value reached by fires of common building combustibles.)

Simultaneously, the fires were creating another problem for the tower. The floors of the 93rd through the 97th stories were being heated both by the hot gases from below and by thermal radiation from the fires on the floor above. On the south side of the building, where the fires were heating the long-span trusses whose SFRM [Sprayed Fire-Resistive Material] had been dislodged, the floors began to sag. In so doing, they began pulling inward on their connections to the south face and to the core columns. Pull-in forces due to the sagging floors did not fail the floor connections in most areas.

## 2.8 9:58:59 A.M. EDT

With no warning that could be discerned in WTC 1, WTC 2 collapsed. The shudder as the more than 250,000 tons of steel, concrete, and furnishings hit the ground was felt well beyond the site. Seismic sensors located 100 miles away recorded the time and intensity of the event. The gigantic concussion was felt by some of the nearly 800 people still in the stairwells in WTC 1. The evacuation rate slowed to half its prior level as a new cloud of dust, smoke, and debris filled the Concourse and the stairwells, and the lights went out. Higher up, no more calls to 9-1-1 originated from above the 91st floor. At 10 a.m., NYPD and FDNY ordered all emergency responders out of WTC 1 and away from the WTC site.

## 2.9 9:59 A.M. TO 10:28 A.M. EDT

A pressure pulse generated by the collapse of WTC 2 appeared to intensify the fires in WTC 1. Within 4 seconds of the collapse of WTC 2, flames burst from the south side windows of the 98th floor. The fires on the north faces of the 92nd, 94th, and 96th floors brightened noticeably. Flames near the south end of the east face of the 92nd and 96th floors also flared. The fires on the east and south faces of the 98th floor already extended out the windows. Those in the WTC 1 stairwells felt a gush of wind. At 10:01 a.m., flames began coming out of the south side of the west face of the 104th floor, three floors higher than any floor where fire had been previously observed and five floors above the highest floor with a major fire. After a rapid growth period, this fire burned intensely up to the time the tower collapsed.

By 10:18 a.m., a substantial pressure pulse inside the building ejected jets of smoke from the 92nd and 94th through 98th floors of the north faces and the 94th and 98th floors of the west face. Fires raged on the south side of the 96th through 99th floors. The sagging of the floors had increased. Although the floors on the north side of the tower had sagged first, they contracted due to cooling when the fires moved toward the south. Now, the south side floors had sagged to the point where the south perimeter columns bowed inward. By 10:23 a.m., the south exterior wall had bowed inward as much as 55 in. At 10:06 a.m., an NYPD aviation unit advised that WTC 1 would come down and that all emergency vehicles should be moved away from it. At 10:20 a.m., observers in NYPD helicopters said that the top of the building was leaning; and at 10:21 a.m., they said that WTC 1 was buckling on the southwest corner and leaning to the south.

The tower was being overwhelmed. Three of the four major structural systems—the core, the floors, and the perimeter walls—were weakening. The south wall became unstable and tried to transfer its remaining load to the weakened core via the hat truss and to adjacent perimeter columns via the spandrels. The entire section of the building above the impact zone began tilting as a rigid block toward the south. The upper section of the building then collapsed onto the floors below. Within 12 seconds, the collapse of WTC 1 had left nothing but rubble.

# Chapter 3: The Account of World Trade Center 2

**3.2** 9:02:59 A.M. EDT

Sixteen and a half minutes after the first impact, five hijackers flew United Airlines (UA) Flight 175, with 9 crew and 51 passengers, into WTC 2 at about 540 mph, about 100 mph faster than AA 11. UA 175 was also a Boeing 767-200ER and had also left Boston, bound for Los Angeles. It flew into WTC 2 carrying about 9,100 gal (62,000 lb) of jet fuel, evenly distributed between the inboard portions of the left and right wing tanks. The cargo bay held about nine tons of luggage, mail, electrical equipment, and food. Combining this with the combustible cabin materials and luggage, the plane brought about 14 tons of solid combustibles into the tower with it.

**3.3** THE IMMEDIATE DAMAGE

The aircraft completely disappeared into the building in a fifth of a second. In response to the force of the collision, the top of the tower swayed 27 in. to the north, taking 2.6 seconds to reach the maximum displacement. UA Flight 175 was heading approximately 15 degrees east of Plan North [approximately 29 degrees clockwise from True North] when it hit the south face of WTC 2 about 23 ft east of the center. The off-center impact twisted the upper part of the building, which vibrated in the north-south direction, along with a twisting motion, with the amplitude decreasing steadily with each oscillation.

The center of the nose of the plane struck at the 81st floor slab. The plane was banked 38 degrees to the left (right wing upward) and was heading slightly (6 degrees) downward from the horizontal. Since the bank angle was steeper than that of AA Flight 11, this entry wound stretched over nine floors, from 77 to 85, rather than eight in WTC 1. The bulk of the impact damage was confined to six floors. Floors 77, 84, and 85 were struck only by the outer extent of the wings. Empty of fuel, the light framing and aluminum sheet of the wing did little damage to the building structure or the SFRM on the columns and trusses on these floors. There were 433 broken windows on the north, east, and south facades. The middle of the left wing hit the 78th floor, severing nine perimeter columns and breaking 19 windows on the south face. The SFRM was stripped from the floor trusses over the same width as the building core. The stripping of insulation from the trusses continued inward across the tenant space and about two-thirds of the way into the core. There was no direct core column damage from the debris on this floor. However, the southeast corner core column was so damaged on the 80th floor that it broke at its splices on the 77th and 83rd floors.

There was heavier damage to the 79th floor. The left engine and the inboard section of the left wing shattered a 25 ft wide section of the center of the floor slab all the way to the core of the building and way to the north end of the core. The damage was most severe on the 80th and 81st floors, hit directly by the fuselage. On the lower floor, a chunk of the floor slab was broken, just above the affected piece of the 79th floor. In addition, a 70 ft deep strip along the east side of the core floor was crushed. The north side floor slab sagged along its eastern end. Ten of the perimeter columns severed on the 79th floor were displaced here also.

Within the building core, ten columns were severed, including many that were severed on the 79th floor. The SFRM was stripped not only from the eastern two-thirds of the core structural elements, nearly to the north wall, but also from most of the trusses on the east tenant space, all the way to the north facade. On the 81st floor, the fuselage pulverized a section of the floor 40 ft wide that extended into the southeast corner of the core. The SFRM and gypsum fire protection on the full depth of the east side of the core and in the entire east side of the tenant space was stripped. The structural damage to the core columns was limited to near the southeast corner, but as mentioned above, the impulses felt here caused damage to the key corner column all the way down to the 78th floor. The right engine passed all the way through the 81st floor, exited from the northeast corner, and damaged the roof of a building on Church Street, before coming to rest some 1,500 ft northeast of WTC 2 near the corner of Murray and Church streets. The right landing gear assembly passed through the 81st floor at the east side of the north face and landed near the engine on the roof of a building on Park Place.

The right engine hit the 82nd floor spandrels about 50 ft from the east edge of the building, crushing part of the 82nd floor slab. Along with the inboard section of the right wing, it severed eight to nine perimeter columns, including some to the east of those severed on the lower floors. The wing caused truss damage up to the southeast corner of the core and severed five columns. As on the 81st floor, the fire protection on the east side of the tenant space and the east side of the core was dislodged. The 83rd floor caught the middle of the starboard wing. The east side floor slab appeared to be dislodged and sagged at least half of the way into the building. The result of the core column damage was that the building core leaned slightly to the southeast above the impact zone. The tendency of the core to lean was resisted by the floors and the hat truss.

The direct impact of the aircraft was over in about 0.6 seconds. The structural and insulation damage was estimated to be:

- 33 exterior columns severed, 1 heavily damaged.
- 10 core columns severed, 1 heavily damaged.
- 39 of 47 core columns stripped of insulation on one or more floors.
- Insulation stripped from trusses covering 80,000 square feet of floor area.

The tower swayed more than one foot back and forth in each direction on the impact floors, about one-third the sway under the high winds for which the building was designed. Nonetheless, just like WTC 1 across the plaza, *WTC 2 absorbed the aircraft strike and remained standing.*

By 9:03 a.m., most of the people in WTC 2 had already left their usual work floors. Nearly 40 percent of all the occupants had left the building, and 90 percent of those who would survive had begun their evacuation. Many of those still on the east side of the impact floors were likely killed or seriously injured by the impact. The same was true for many of those on the 78th floor sky lobby, who were deciding on a course of action, waiting for the express elevators to transport them to the ground floor, or attempting to return to their offices. Those on the west side of the building were less seriously affected. In calls to 9-1-1, they reported fallen ceiling tiles, collapsed walls, jet fuel, heat, smoke, and fire.

This aircraft had also severed the pipes that fed the automatic sprinklers and destroyed all elevator service to the impact floors. But, unlike AA Flight 11, the off-center strike of UA Flight 175 had left one of the three stairways passable, Stairway A on the north side of the building core. It was well west of the aircraft strike center and partially protected by elevator machinery and the long dimension of the building core.

When the aircraft struck WTC 2, emergency responders had already been dispatched to the WTC site, and the initial surge of emergency responder radio had subsided to a level approximately three times that of normal operations. However, the radio traffic volume was still at a level where approximately one-third to one-half of the radio communications was not understandable.

## 3.4 THE JET FUEL

Within about 0.5 seconds, dust and debris flew out of windows on the east and north faces. Several small fireballs of atomized jet fuel burst from windows on the east face of the 81st and 82nd floors, coalescing into a single, large fireball that spanned the entire face. A tenth of a second later, fire appeared in the dust clouds ejected from the south face of the 79th, 81st, and 82nd floors. Almost simultaneously, three fireballs came from the east side of the north face. The largest came from the 80th through 82nd floors. A second, somewhat smaller one came from the same floors on the northeast corner of the building. The smallest emerged from the 79th floor. No dust or fireballs came from the west face.

As in WTC 1, less than 15 percent of the jet fuel burned in the spray cloud inside the building. Roughly 10 percent to 25 percent was consumed in the fireballs outside the building. Thus, well over half of the jet fuel remained after the initial fireballs.

The rapid burning of the jet fuel inside the building created an overpressure that was estimated at 2 psi [pounds per square inch] to 3 psi for 0.5 to 2 seconds. For a window and frame of more than 10 square feet, this amounts to more than 3,000 pounds of force, more than enough to break windows.

Photographs of the north and east faces appear to show hanging floor slabs where the fireballs had been ejected from the building. Based on the failure of the truss seat connections, NIST estimated that the static capacity of an undamaged floor was 4.8 psi against uplift pressure and 4.4 psi against downward pressure over the entire floor. It is not unreasonable that a combination of physical damage from the impact and overpressure from the fireballs caused the partial collapse of these floor slabs.

## 3.5 9:03 A.M. TO 9:36 A.M. EDT

The fireballs burned for 10 seconds, extending almost 200 ft out from the north, east, and south faces. Having consumed the aerosol fuel, the flames then receded. For the next half hour, small fires were burning in and near the aircraft impact cavity on the south side of the building. There were vigorous fires on the east side of the 80th through 83rd floors, especially on the northeast end of the 81st and 82nd floors, where the aircraft had bulldozed the office desks and chairs and added its own combustibles. In addition to the ample supply of fuel, these fires had access to plenty of air, as numerous windows on the east face had been blown out by the impact or fireball. They would continue to burn as long as the building stood.

Between 9:30 a.m. and 9:34 a.m., there were several large bursts of smoke from the 79th and 80th floors of the north face, possibly resulting from the ignition of pools of jet fuel that had settled there, or from shifting of dislodged floor slabs elsewhere. Dire structural changes were occurring in the building interior. Core columns, including the massive southeast corner column, had been severed by the aircraft. The loads from these columns had been redistributed to other, intact core columns and to the east exterior wall. The core leaned to the south and east, restrained from further movement by the east and south walls through the floors and the hat truss.

The fires were weakening the structure in a manner different from WTC 1. First, the severed core columns in the southeast corner led to the failure of some column splices to the hat truss. Nonetheless, the hat truss continued to transfer loads from the core to the perimeter walls. Second, the overall load redistribution increased the loads on the east wall. Third, the increasing temperatures over time on the long-span floors on the east side had led to significant sagging on the 79th through 83rd floors, resulting in an inward pull force. Fourth, within 18 minutes of the aircraft impact, there was inward bowing of the east perimeter columns as a result of the floors sagging. As the exposure time to the high temperatures lengthened, these pull-in forces from the sagging floors increased the inward bowing of the east perimeter columns.

## 3.6 9:36 A.M. TO 9:58 A.M. EDT

By 9:58 a.m., all but eleven of the occupants who had been below the impact floors had left the building and crossed the street to safety. The fires continued to burn in the east half of the building. At 9:55 a.m., firefighters communicated that they had reached floor 55 of WTC 2, one of the few calls for which a record survived indicating how high the responders had reached. Before WTC 2 collapsed, firefighters had reached the 78th floor by using the single functioning elevator to the 40th floor and then climbing the stairs.

The physical condition of the tower had deteriorated seriously. The inward bowing of columns on the east wall spread along the east face. The east wall lost its ability to support gravity loads, and, consequently, redistributed the loads to the weakened core through the hat truss and to the adjacent north and south walls through the spandrels. But the loads could not be supported by the weakened structure, and the entire section of the building above the impact zone began tilting as a rigid block to the east and south. Column failure continued from the east wall around the corners to the north and south faces. The top of the building continued to tilt to the east and south, as, at 9:58:59 a.m., WTC 2 began to collapse.

## 6.14.4 STRUCTURAL RESPONSE OF THE WTC TOWERS TO FIRE WITHOUT IMPACT OR INSULATION DAMAGE

To complete the assessment of the relative roles of aircraft impact and ensuing fires, NIST examined whether an intense, but conventional, fire, occurring without the aircraft impact, could have led to the collapse of a WTC tower, were it in the same condition as it was on September 10, 2001. The characteristics of such an intense, conventional fire could have been:

- Ignition on a single floor by a small bomb or other explosion. If arson were involved, there might have been multiple small fires ignited on a few floors.
- Air supply determined by the building ventilation system.
- Moderate fire growth rate. In the case of arson, several gallons of an accelerant might have been applied to the building combustibles, igniting the equivalent of several workstations.
- Water supply to the sprinklers and standpipes maliciously compromised.
- Intact structural insulation and interior walls.

The four cases described in this chapter represented fires that were far more severe than this:

- About 10,000 gallons of jet fuel were sprayed into multiple stories, quickly and simultaneously igniting hundreds of workstations.
- The aircraft and subsequent fireballs created large open areas in the building exterior through which air could flow to support the fires.
- The impact and debris removed the insulation from a large number of structural elements that were then subjected to the heat from the fires.

Additional findings from the investigation showed that:

- Both the results of the multiple workstation experiments and the simulations of the WTC fires showed that the combustibles in a given location, if undisturbed by the aircraft impact, would have been almost fully burned out in about 20 min.

- In the simulations, none of the columns and trusses for which the insulation was intact reached temperatures at which significant loss of strength occurred.
- Both WTC 1 and WTC 2 were stable after the aircraft impact, standing for 102 min and 56 min, respectively. The global analyses with structural impact damage showed that both towers had considerable reserve capacity. This was confirmed by analysis of the post-impact vibration of WTC 2, the more severely damaged building, where the damaged tower oscillated at a period nearly equal to the first mode period calculated for the undamaged structure.
- Computer simulations, supported by the results of large-scale fire tests and furnace testing of floor subsystems, showed that insulated structural steel, when coated with the average installed insulation thickness of ¾ in., would have withstood the heat from nearby fires for a longer time than the burnout time of the combustibles. Simulations also showed that variations in thickness resulting from normal application, even with occasional gaps in coverage, would not have changed this result.

From these, NIST concluded:

- An intense, conventional fire, in the absence of structural and insulation damage, would not have led to the collapse of a WTC tower.
- The existing condition of the insulation prior to aircraft impact, which was found to be mostly intact, and the insulation thickness on the WTC floor system did not play a significant role in initiating collapse of the towers.
- The towers would not have collapsed under the combined effects of aircraft impact and the subsequent multifloor fires if the insulation had not been widely dislodged or had been only minimally dislodged by aircraft impact.

## 8.3.2 STRUCTURAL STEELS

- Fourteen different strengths of steel were specified in the structural engineering plans, but only 12 steels of different strength were actually used in construction due to an upgrade of two steels. Ten different steel companies fabricated structural elements for the towers, using steel supplied from at least eight different suppliers. Four fabricators supplied the major structural elements of the 9th to the 107th floors. Material substitutions of higher strength steels were not uncommon in the perimeter columns and floor trusses.

- About 87 percent of the tested steel specimens (columns, trusses, and bolts) met or exceeded the required yield strengths specified in design documents. About 13 percent had NIST measured strengths that were slightly lower than the design values, but this may have arisen from mechanical damage during the collapse, the natural variability of structural steel, and slight differences between the NIST and original mill test report testing protocols.

- The safety of the WTC towers on September 11, 2001, was most likely not affected by the fraction of steel that, according to NIST testing, was modestly below the required minimum yield strength. The typical factors of safety in allowable stress design were capable of accommodating the measured property variations below the minimum.

- The pre-collapse photographic analysis showed that 16 recovered exterior panels were exposed to fire prior to collapse of WTC 1. None of the nine recovered panels from within the fire floors of WTC 2 were observed to have been directly exposed to fire.

- None of the recovered steel samples showed evidence of exposure to temperatures above 600 °C [1,112 °F] for as long as 15 minutes. This was based on NIST annealing studies that established the set of time and temperature conditions necessary to alter the steel microstructure. These results provide some confirmation of the thermal modeling of the structures, since none of the samples were from zones where such heating was predicted.

- Only three of the recovered samples of exterior panels reached temperatures in excess of 250 °C [482 °F] during the fires or after the collapse. This was based on a method developed by NIST to characterize maximum temperatures experienced by steel members through observations of paint cracking.

- Perimeter columns exposed to fire had a great tendency for local buckling of the inner web; a similar correlation did not exist for weld failure.

- Observations of the recovered steel provided significant guidance for modeling the damage from the aircraft impact with the towers.

- For the perimeter columns struck by the aircraft, fractures of the plates in areas away from a welded joint exhibited ductile behavior (necking and thinning away from the fracture) under very high strain rates. Conversely, fractures occurring next to a welded joint exhibited little or no ductile characteristics.

- There was no evidence to indicate that the type of joining method, materials, or welding procedures were improper. The welds appeared to perform as intended.
- The failure mode of spandrel connections on perimeter panels differed above and below the impact zone. Spandrel connections on exterior panels at or above the impact zone were more likely to fail by bolt tear out. For those exterior panels below the impact zone, there was a higher propensity for the spandrels to be ripped off from the panels. This may be due to shear failures as the weight of the building came down on these lower panels. There was no difference in failure mode for the spandrel connections whether the exterior panels were exposed to fire or not.
- With the exception of the mechanical floors, the perimeter panel column splices failed by fracture of the bolts. At mechanical floors, where splices were welded in addition to being bolted, the majority of the splices did not fail.
- Core columns failed at both splice connection and by fracture of the columns themselves.
- The damage to truss seats on perimeter panels differed above and below the impact zone in both towers. The majority of recovered perimeter panel floor truss connectors (perimeter seats) below the impact floors were either missing or bent downward. Above this level, the failure modes were more randomly distributed.
- In the floor trusses, a large majority of the electric resistance welds at the web-to-chord connections failed. The floor truss and the perimeter panel floor truss connectors typically failed at welds and bolts.
- The NIST-measured properties of the steels (strain rate, impact toughness, high-temperature yield, and tensile strengths) were similar to literature values for other construction steels of the WTC era.
- The creep behavior of the steels could be modeled by scaling WTC-era literature data using room temperature tensile strength ratios.

## 8.3.5 STRUCTURAL RESPONSE AND COLLAPSE ANALYSIS

- The core columns were weakened significantly by the aircraft impact damage and thermal effects. Thermal effects dominated the weakening of WTC 1. As the fires moved from the north to the south side of the core, the core was weakened over time by significant creep strains on the south side of the core. Aircraft impact damage dominated the weakening of WTC 2. With the impact damage, the core subsystem leaned to the southeast and was supported by the south and east perimeter walls via the hat truss and floors. As the core weakened, it redistributed loads to the perimeter walls through the hat truss and floors. Additional axial loads redistributed to the exterior columns from the core were not significant (only about 20 percent to 25 percent on average) as the exterior columns were loaded to approximately 20 percent of their capacity before the aircraft impact.

- The primary role of the floors in the collapse of the towers was to provide inward pull forces that induced inward bowing of perimeter columns (south face of WTC 1; east face of WTC 2). Sagging floors continued to support floor loads as they pulled inward on the perimeter columns. There would have been no inward pull forces if the floor connections had failed and disconnected.

- Column buckling over an extended region of the perimeter face ultimately triggered the global system collapse as the loads could not be redistributed through the hat truss to the already weakened building core. As the exterior wall buckled (south face for WTC 1 and east face for WTC 2), the column instability propagated to adjacent faces and caused the initiation of the building collapse. Perimeter wall buckling was induced by a combination of thermal weakening of the columns, inward pull forces from sagging floors, and to a much lesser degree, additional axial loads redistributed from the core.

- The insulation damage estimates were conservative as they ignored possibly damaged and dislodged insulation in a much larger region that was not in the direct path of the debris but was subject to strong vibrations during and after the aircraft impact. A robust criterion to generate a coherent pattern of vibration-induced dislodging could not be established to estimate the larger region of damaged insulation.

- For WTC 1, partitions were damaged and insulation was dislodged by direct debris impact over five floors (floors 94, 95, 96, 97, and 98) and included most of the north floor areas in front of the core, the core, and central regions of the south floor areas, and on some floors, extended to the south wall.

- For WTC 2, partitions were damaged and insulation was dislodged by direct debris impact over six floors (floors 79, 80, 81, 82, and 83) and included the south floor area in front of the core, the central and east regions of the core, and most of the east floor area, and extended to the north wall.

- The adhesive strength of CAFCO BLAZE-SHIELD DC/F to steel coated with primer paint was found to be one-third to one-half of the adhesive strength to steel that had not been coated with primer paint. The SFRM products used in the WTC towers were applied to steel components with primer paint.
- The average thickness of the original thermal insulation on the floor trusses was estimated to be 0.75 in. with a standard deviation of 0.3 in. The average thickness of the upgraded thermal insulation was estimated to be 2.5 in. with a standard deviation of 0.6 in. Based on finite element simulations, the thermal analyses for determining temperature histories of structural components used a thermally equivalent thickness of 0.6 in. and 2.2 in. for the original and upgraded insulation, respectively. For thermal analyses of the perimeter columns, spandrel beams, core beams, and core columns, the insulation on these elements was set to the specified thickness, due to a lack of field measurements.
- Based on four Standard Fire Tests conducted for various length scales, insulation thickness, and end restraints, the floor assemblies were shown to be capable of sagging without collapsing and supported their full design load under standard fire conditions for 2 hours or more without failure.
- For assemblies with a ¾ in. SFRM thickness, the 17 ft assembly's fire rating was 2 hours; the 35 ft assembly's rating was 1½ hours. This result raised the question of whether or not a fire rating of a 17 ft floor assembly is scalable to the longer spans in the WTC towers.
- The specimen with ½ in. SFRM thickness and a 17 ft span would not have met the 2-hour requirement of the NYC Building Code.
- There is far greater knowledge of how fires influence structures in 2005 than there was in the 1960s. The analysis tools available to calculate the response of structures to fires are also far better now than they were when the WTC towers were designed and built.

## APPENDIX C

# FINAL REPORT ON WORLD TRADE CENTER BUILDING 7

T he following material is abridged and excerpted from the *Final Report on the Collapse of World Trade Center Building 7*, also known as NCSTAR 1A, which was prepared for the National Institute of Standards and Technology (NIST), a nonregulatory agency of the U.S. Department of Commerce's Technology Administration.

This report describes how the fires that followed from the impact of debris from the collapse of WTC 1 (the north tower) led to the collapse of WTC 7. Also in this report is a summary of how NIST reached its conclusions. NIST complemented in-house expertise with private sector technical experts; accumulated copious documents, photographs, and videos of the disaster; conducted first-person interviews of building occupants and emergency responders; analyzed the evacuation and emergency response operations in and around WTC 7; performed computer simulations of WTC 7 on September 11, 2001; and combined the knowledge gained into a probable collapse sequence.

This report was released in November of 2008. To read the complete document, go to http://wtc.nist.gov/pubs. Extensive details are found in the companion documents to this report, NIST NCSTAR 1-9 and NIST NCSTAR 1-9A.

# Executive Summary

## E.3 SUMMARY OF FINDINGS

The fires in WTC 7 were ignited as a result of the impact of debris from the collapse of WTC 1, which was approximately 110 m (350 ft) to the south. The debris also caused structural damage to the southwest exterior of WTC 7, primarily between Floors 7 to 17. The fires were ignited on at least 10 floors; however, only the fires on Floors 7 through 9 and 11 through 13 grew and lasted until the time of the building collapse. These uncontrolled fires had characteristics similar to those that have occurred previously in tall buildings. Their growth and spread were consistent with ordinary building contents fires. Had a water supply for the automatic sprinkler system been available and had the sprinkler system operated as designed, it is likely that the fires in WTC 7 would have been controlled and the collapse prevented. However, the collapse of WTC 7 highlights the importance of designing fire-resistant structures for situations where sprinklers are not present, do not function (e.g., due to disconnected or impaired water supply), or are overwhelmed.

Eventually, the fires reached the northeast region of the building. The probable collapse sequence that caused the global collapse of WTC 7 involved the initiation of the buckling of a critical interior column in that vicinity. This column had become unsupported over nine stories after initial local fire-induced damage led to a cascade of local floor failures. The buckling of this column led to a vertical progression of floor failures up to the roof, and led to the buckling of adjacent interior columns to the south of the critical column. An east-to-west horizontal progression of interior column buckling followed, due to loss of lateral support to adjacent columns, forces exerted by falling debris, and load redistribution from other buckled columns. The exterior columns then buckled as the failed building core moved downward, redistributing its loads lo the exterior columns. Global collapse occurred as the entire building above the buckled region moved downward as a single unit. This was a fire-induced progressive collapse, also known as disproportionate collapse, which is defined as the spread of local damage, from an initiating event, from element to element, eventually resulting in the collapse of an entire structure, or a disproportionately large part of it.

Factors contributing to the building failure were: thermal expansion occurring at temperatures hundreds of degrees below those typically considered in design practice for establishing structural fire resistance ratings; significant magnification of thermal expansion effects due to the long-span floors, which are common in office buildings in widespread use; connections that were designed to resist gravity loads, but not thermally induced lateral loads; and a structural system that was not designed to prevent fire-induced progressive collapse.

Within the building were: emergency electric power generators, whose fuel supply tanks lay in and under the building. However, fuel oil fires did not play a role in the collapse of WTC 7. The worst-case scenarios associated with fires being fed by the ruptured fuel lines (a) could not have been sustained long enough, or could not have generated sufficient heat, to raise the temperature of the critical interior column to the point of significant loss of strength or stiffness, or (b) would have produced large amounts of visible smoke that would have emanated from the exhaust louvers. No such smoke discharge was observed.

Simulations of hypothetical blast events show that no blast event played a role in the collapse of WTC 7. NIST concluded that blast events did not occur, and found no evidence whose explanation required invocation of a blast event. Blast from the smallest charge capable of failing a single critical column would have resulted in a sound level of 130 dB to 140 dB at a distance of at least half a mile. There were no witness reports of such a loud noise, nor was such a noise heard on the audio tracks of video recordings of the WTC 7 collapse.

There were no serious injuries or fatalities, because the estimated 4.000 occupants of WTC 7 reacted to the airplane impacts on the two WTC towers and began evacuating before there was significant damage to WTC 7. The occupants were able to use both the elevators and the stairs, which were as yet not damaged, obstructed, or smoke-filled. Evacuation of the building took just over an hour. The potential for injuries to people leaving the building was mitigated by building management personnel holding the occupants in the lobby until they identified an exit path that was safe from the debris falling from WTC 1. The decision not to continue evaluating the building and not to fight the fires was made hours before the building collapsed, so no emergency responders were in or near the building when the collapse occurred.

The design of WTC 7 was generally consistent with the New York City Building Code of 1968 (NYCBC), with which, by PANYNJ policy, it was to comply. The installed thicknesses of the thermal insulation was consistent with the rating required by the NYCBC. The stairwells were narrower than those required by the NYCBC, but, combined with the elevators, were adequate for a timely evacuation on September 11, 2001, since the number of building occupants was only about half that expected during normal business hours.

The collapse of WTC 7 could not have been prevented without controlling the fires before most of the combustible building contents were consumed. There were two sources of water (gravity fed overhead tanks and the city water main) for the standpipe and automatic sprinkler systems serving Floor 21 and above, and some of the early fires on those upper floors might have actually been controlled in this manner. However, consistent with the NYCBC, both the primary and back-up source of water for the sprinkler system in the lower 20 floors of WTC 7 was the city water main. Since the collapses of the WTC towers had damaged the water main, there was no secondary supply of water available (such as from the gravity-fed overhead tanks that supplied water to Floor 21 and above) to control those fires that eventually led to the building collapse.

Other than initiating the fires in WTC 7, the damage from the debris WTC 1 had little effect on initiating the collapse of WTC 7. The building withstood debris impact damage that resulted in seven exterior columns being severed and subsequently withstood fires involving typical office combustibles on several floors for almost seven hours. The debris damaged the spray-applied fire resistive material that was applied to the steel columns, girders, and beams, only in the vicinity of the structural damage from the collapse of WTC 1. This was near the west side of the south face of the building and was far removed from the buckled column that initiated the collapse. Even without the structural damage, WTC 7 would have collapsed from fires having the same characteristics as those experienced on September 11, 2001. The transfer elements such as trusses, girders, and cantilever overhangs that were used to support the office building over the Con Edison substation did not play a significant role in the collapse of WTC 7.

# Chapter 1: The New York City World Trade Center Building 7

## 1.2.3 THE STRUCTURE

WTC 7 was an irregular trapezoid, approximately 100 m (329 ft) long on the north face and 75 m (247 ft) long on the south face, 44 m (144 ft) wide, and 186 m (610 ft) tall. The 47-story building contained approximately 200,000 m2 (2 million ft2) of floor area. A typical floor was similar in size to a football field. The gross floor area was about 75 percent of that contained in the Empire State Building. As shown in Figure 1–3, about half of WTC 7 rose outside the footprint of the Con Edison substation. Structurally, WTC 7 consisted of four "tiers."

- The lowest four floors housed two two-story lobbies, one each on the center of the south side of the 1st and 3rd floors. The north side of the 1st and 2nd stories was the Con Edison substation. The remainder of the north, east, and west sides of these four stories was conference space, offices, a cafeteria, etc.
- Floors 5 and 6 were mechanical spaces. Within the volume bounded by the 5th floor slab and the 7th floor slab were three transfer trusses and a series of eight cantilever transfer girders. As their names indicate, these steel assemblies distributed the load of the upper floors of WTC 7 onto the structural frame of the Con Edison substation and the structure of the lowest four floors of WTC 7.
- Floors 7 through 45 were tenant floors, all structurally similar to each other. The exception was a reinforcing belt truss around Floors 22 and 23.
- The 46th and 47th floors, while mainly tenant floors, were structurally reinforced to support special loads, such as the cooling towers and the water tanks for fire suppression.

The structural frame was designed to distribute the weight of the building (gravity loads) and resist (lateral) wind loads. The frame included columns, floor assemblies, spandrel beams, girders, and transfer elements.

From the 7 floor to the 47 floor, WTC 7 was supported by 24 interior columns and 58 perimeter columns (numbered 1 through 57, plus 14A, which was located near the south end of the west face). Twenty-one of the interior columns (numbered 58 through 78) formed a rectangular building core, which was offset toward the west of the building. The remaining three interior columns (79, 80, and 81) were particularly large, as they provided support for the long floor spans on the east side of the building.

In the final design of WTC 7, the layout of the columns did not align with the building foundation and the Con Edison columns. Therefore, a set of column transfers were constructed within the volume bounded by the 5th and 7th floor slabs.

## 1.2.6 THE COMBUSTIBLE CONTENTS

The layout of most of the floors featured clusters of workstations, or cubicles, throughout the space surrounding the building core. Often, there were walled offices at the perimeter. The layout in Figure 1–8 is indicative of these floors. While there were almost certainly different types of workstations in the building, they were all fundamentally similar. Each cubicle typically was bounded on four sides by privacy panels, with a single entrance opening. Within the area defined by the panels was a self-contained workspace: desktop (almost always a wood product, generally with a laminated finish), file storage, bookshelves, carpeting, chair, etc. Presumably there were a variety of amounts and locations of paper, both exposed on the work surfaces and contained within the file cabinets and bookshelves.

The combustible fuel load for these open landscaped floors was dominated by the workstations. The architectural drawings showed densities of workstations similar to those on most of the fire floors in the WTC towers. The estimated combustible fuel load for these floors was about 20 kg/m2 (4 lb/ft2). Simulations of the fires with a higher combusted fuel load resulted in poor agreement with the observed fire spread rates.

On the 11 and 12 floors, which will be seen later to have been the sites of significant and sustained fires, the mass of additional paper materials was described as very high. As indicated in NIST NCSTAR 1-9, Chapter 3, the Investigation Team estimated a combustible fuel load of approximately 32 kg/m3 (6.4 lb/ft2). Simulations of the fires with a lower combustible fuel load showed little effect on the rate of fire progression.

Unlike the case for the two WTC towers, there was no widespread spraying of jet fuel to ignite numerous workstations or offices simultaneously. Rather, in the earlier hours of the fires, following the debris impact due to the collapse of WTC 1, the fire would have spread from one individual workstation or office to another. Thus, the fire spread would have been dependent on the office walls, the specific spacing of the cubicles, the ease of ignition of the furnishings, their combustible mass, and the extent of surface occlusion by foreign matter.

# Chapter 2: The Account of WTC 7

## 2.4 THE PROBABLE COLLAPSE SEQUENCE

The following is the NIST account of how the fires in WTC 7 most likely led to the building's collapse.

The collapse of WTC 1 damaged seven exterior columns, between Floors 7 and 17 of the south and west faces of WTC 7. It also ignited fires on at least 10 floors between Floors 7 and 30, and the fires burned out of control on Floors 7 to 9 and 11 to 13. Fires on these six floors grew and spread since they were not extinguished either by the automatic sprinkler system or by FDNY, because water was not available in WTC 7. Fires were generally concentrated on the east and north sides of the northeast region beginning at about 3 p.m. to 4 p.m.

As the fires progressed, some of the structural steel began to heat. According to the generally accepted test standard, ASTM E-119, one of the criteria for establishing the fire resistance rating for a steel column or floor beam is derived from the time at which, during a standard fire exposure, the average column temperature exceeds 538 °C (1000 °F) or the average floor beam temperature exceeds 593 °C (1100 °F). These are temperatures at which there is significant loss of steel strength and stiffness. Due to the effectiveness of the SFRM, the highest column temperatures in WTC 7 only reached an estimated 300 °C (570 °F), and only on the east side of the building did the floor beams reach or exceed about 600 °C (1100 °F). The heat from these uncontrolled fires caused thermal expansion of the steel beams on the lower floors of the east side of WTC 7, primarily at or below 400 °C (750 °F), damaging the floor framing on multiple floors.

The initiating local failure that began the probable WTC 7 collapse sequence was the buckling of Column 79. This buckling arose from a process that occurred at temperatures at or below approximately 400 °C (750 °F), which are well below the temperatures considered in current practice for determining fire resistance ratings associated with significant loss of steel strength. When steel (or any other metal) is heated, it expands. If thermal expansion in steel beams is resisted by columns or other steel members, forces develop in the structural members that can result in buckling of beams or failures of connections.

Fire-induced thermal expansion of the floor system surrounding Column 79 led to the collapse of Floor 13, which triggered a cascade of floor failures. In this case, the floor beams on the east side of the building expanded enough that they pushed the girder spanning between Columns 79 and 44 to the west on the 13th floor. (See Figure 1–5 for column numbering and the locations of girders and beams.) This movement was enough for the girder to walk off of its support at Column 79.

The unsupported girder and other local fire-induced damage caused Floor 13 to collapse, beginning a cascade of floor failures down to the 5th floor. Many of these floors had already been at least partially weakened by the fires in the vicinity of Column 79. This left Column 79 with insufficient lateral support, and as a consequence, the column buckled eastward, becoming the initial local failure for collapse initiation.

Due to the buckling of Column 79 between Floors 5 and 14, the upper section of Column 79 began to descend. The downward movement of Column 79 led to the observed kink in the east penthouse, and its subsequent descent. The cascading failures of the lower floors surrounding Column 79 led to increased unsupported length in, falling debris impact on, and loads being re-distributed to adjacent columns; and Column 80 and then Column 81 buckled as well. All the floor connections to these three columns, as well as to the exterior columns, failed, and the floors fell on the east side of the building. The exterior façade on the east quarter of the building was just a hollow shell.

The failure of the interior columns then proceeded toward the west. Truss 2 (Figure 1–6) failed, hit by the debris from the falling floors. This caused Column 77 and Column 78 to fail, followed shortly by Column 76. Each north-south line of three core columns then buckled in succession from east to west, due to loss of lateral support from floor system failures, to the forces exerted by falling debris, which tended to push the columns westward, and to the loads redistributed to them from the buckled columns. Within seconds, the entire building core was buckling.

The global collapse of WTC 7 was underway. The shell of exterior columns buckled between the 7 and 14th floors, as loads were redistributed to these columns due to the downward movement of the building core and the floors. The entire building above the buckled-column region then moved downward as a single unit, completing the global collapse sequence.

# Chapter 3: Deriving the Probable Collapse Sequence

## 3.1 GATHERING OF EVIDENCE

Similar to the investigation into the collapse of the WTC towers, data for WTC 7 were collected from a number of sources and reviewed. Much of the information on WTC 7 was gathered and published during the reconstruction of the collapses of the towers. Comparison of the various building codes in use at the time of construction was the subject of NIST NCSTAR 1-1E. Details of the fire safety provisions and systems were published in NIST NCSTAR reports 1-1D, 1-1G, 1-1I, 1-4B, 1-4C, and 1-4D. The emergency power systems were described in NIST NCSTAR 1-1J. Properties of the structural steels used in the construction were the subject of NIST NCSTAR 1-3D and NIST NCSTAR 1-3E. The SFRM properties were presented in NCSTAR 1-6A. Much of the activities of the emergency responders was reported in NIST NCSTAR 1-8. A description of the collection and cataloguing of the photographic and videographic evidence appeared in NIST NCSTAR 1-5A. This included visuals of debris impact damage and fire spread subsequent to collapse of the WTC towers. Additional imagery was collected subsequent to the previously reported library. While not as plentiful as the imagery for the WTC towers, the cumulative WTC 7 evidence was sufficient to guide the reconstruction of the day's events.

As with the WTC towers, much of the information specific to the WTC 7 building construction was lost with the destruction of the WTC site. Nonetheless, copious information was obtained from drawings and specifications, reports, and available records from The Port Authority, Silverstein Properties, and a number of contractors that had worked on the design, construction, or modifications of WTC 7. The documents included erection and fabrication shop drawings of the building, which provided detailed information about the floor and column connections. Information and documents regarding the layout of the building interior were obtained from WTC 7 tenants. Staff of the occupying organizations and Silverstein Properties staff were also interviewed to gain additional insights into the layout, furnishing, and overall fuel loads. Additional interviews with emergency responders and building officials, along with tapes of radio transmissions from September 11, 2001, provided accounts of the human activity inside the building and around the WTC site.

# Chapter 4: Principal Findings

**4.2** SUMMARY

Objective 1: Determine why and how WTC 7 collapsed.

- WTC 7 withstood debris impact damage that resulted in seven exterior columns being severed and subsequently withstood fires involving typical office combustibles on several floors for almost seven hours.
- The collapse of WTC 7 represents the first known instance of the total collapse of a tall building primarily due to fires. The collapse could not have been prevented without controlling the fires before most of the combustible building contents were consumed.
- WTC 7 collapsed due to uncontrolled fires with characteristics similar to previous fires in tall buildings. The fires in WTC 7 were similar to those that have occurred in several tall buildings (One New York

Plaza, 1970, First Interstate Bank, 1988, and One Meridian Plaza, 1991) where the automatic sprinklers did not function or were not present. However, because of differences between their structural designs and that of WTC 7, these three buildings did not collapse. Fires for the range of combustible contents in WTC 7—20 kg/m$^2$ (4.0 lb/ft$^2$) on Floors 7 to 9 and 32 kg/m$^2$ (6.4 lb/ft$^2$) on Floors 11 to 13—persisted in any given location for approximately 20 min to 30 min. Had a water supply for the automatic sprinkler system been available and had the sprinkler system operated as designed, it is likely that fires in VVTC 7 would have been controlled and the collapse prevented.

- The probable collapse sequence that caused the global collapse of WTC 7 was initiated by the buckling of Column 79, which was unsupported over nine stories, after local fire-induced damage led to a cascade of floor failures. The buckling of Column 79 led to a vertical progression of floor failures up to the east penthouse and to the buckling of Columns 80 and 81. An east-to-west horizontal progression of interior column buckling followed, due to loss of lateral support to adjacent columns, forces exerted by falling debris, and load redistribution from other buckled columns. The exterior columns then buckled as the failed building core moved downward, redistributing its loads to the exterior columns. Global collapse occurred as the entire building above the buckled region moved downward as a single unit.

- The collapse of WTC 7 was a fire-induced progressive collapse. The American Society of Civil Engineers defines progressive collapse—also known as disproportionate collapse—as the spread of local damage, from an initiating event, from element to element, eventually resulting in the collapse of an entire structure or a disproportionately large part of it (ASCE 7-05). Despite extensive thermal weakening of connections and buckled floor beams of Floors 8 to 14, fire-induced damage in the floor framing surrounding Column 79 over nine stories was the determining factor causing the buckling of Column 79 and, thereby, initiating progressive collapse. This is the first known instance where fire-induced local damage (i.e., buckling failure of Column 79: one of 82 columns in WTC 7) led to the collapse of an entire tall building.

- WTC 7 was prone to classic progressive collapse in the absence of debris impact and fire-induced damage when a section of Column 79 between Floors 11 and 13 was removed. The collapse sequence demonstrated a vertical and horizontal progression of failure upon the removal of the Column 79 section, followed by buckling of exterior columns, which led to the collapse of the entire building.

- Neither the transfer elements (trusses, girders, and cantilever overhangs) nor the "strong" floors (Floors 5 and 7) played a significant role in the collapse of WTC 7. Neither did the Con Edison substation play a significant role in the collapse of WTC 7.

- There was no evidence to suggest that there was damage to the SFRM that was applied to the steel columns, girders, and beams, except in the vicinity of the structural damage from the collapse of WTC 1, which was near the west side of the south face of the building.

- Even without the initial structural damage caused by debris impact from the collapse of WTC 1, WTC 7 would have collapsed from fires having the same characteristics as those experienced on September 11, 2001.

- Early fires in the southwest region of the building did not play a role in the collapse of WTC 7. The fires in this region were not severe enough to heat the structure significantly; and, unlike the northeast region where collapse initiated, there were no columns supporting long span floors in the southwest region.

- The observed descent time of the upper 18 stories of the north face of WTC 7 (the floors clearly visible in the video evidence) was 40 percent greater than the computed free fall time. A more detailed analysis of the descent of the north face found three stages: (1) a slow descent with acceleration less than that of gravity that corresponded to the buckling of the exterior columns at the lower floors, (2) a freefall descent over approximately eight stories at gravitational acceleration for approximately 2.25 s, and (3) a decreasing acceleration as the face encountered resistance from the structure below.

- Diesel fuel fires did not play a role in the collapse of WTC 7. The worst-case scenarios associated with fires being fed by the ruptured fuel lines (a) could not have been sustained long enough, or could not have generated sufficient heat to raise the temperature of a critical column (i.e., Column 79) to the point of significant loss of strength or stiffness, or (b) would have produced large amounts of visible smoke that would have emanated the exhaust louvers. No such smoke discharge was observed.

- Blast events did not play a role in the collapse of WTC 7. Based on visual and audio evidence and the use of specialized computer modeling to simulate hypothetical blast events, NIST concluded that blast events did not occur, and found no evidence whose explanation required invocation of a blast event. Blast from the smallest charge capable of failing a critical column (i.e., Column 79) would have resulted in a sound level of 130 dB to 140 dB at a distance of at least half a mile if unobstructed by surrounding buildings (such as along Greenwich Street or West Broadway). This sound level is consistent with standing next to a jet plane engine and more than 10 times louder than being in front of the speakers at a rock concert. There were no reports of such a loud noise, nor was such a noise heard on the audio tracks of video recordings of the WTC 7 collapse.

# PENTAGON BUILDING REPORT

T he following excerpts are from *The Pentagon Building Performance Report*, an investigation commissioned by the American Society of Civil Engineers (ASCE) and conducted by a team of experts to assess the structural performance of the building after it was struck by American Airlines Flight 77 on September 11, 2001. The report was released in January 2003. To read the complete text, go to http://fire.nist.gov/bfrlpubs/build03/art017.html.

## The Pentagon Building

### PERFORMANCE REPORT AUTHORS

**Paul F. Mlakar**, Ph.D., P.E.,
Lead Technical Director
U.S. Army Corps of Engineers

**Donald O. Dusenberry**, P.E.
Principal
Simpson Gumpertz & Heger, Inc.

**James R. Harris**, Ph.D., P.E.
Principal
J.R. Harris & Company

**Gerald Haynes**, P.E.
Fire Protection Engineer
Bureau of Alcohol, Tobacco, and Firearms

**Long T. Phan**, Ph.D., P.E.
Research Structural Engineer
National Institute of Standards and Technology

**Mete A. Sozen**, Ph.D., S.E.
Kettelhut Distinguished Professor of Structural Engineering
Purdue University

## 2.1 DOCUMENTS FOR ORIGINAL CONSTRUCTION

The Pentagon is in the midst of a major renovation program, and the work is phased in five "wedges" that do not correspond to either the sections or the areas. Each wedge is centered on a building vertex and consists of the portion of the building between the midpoint of adjacent sides. The renovation of Wedge 1 began in 1999 and was essentially complete at the time of the crash.

The original structural system, including the roof, was entirely cast-in-place reinforced concrete using normal-weight aggregate. Most of the structure used a specified concrete strength of 2,500 psi [pounds per square inch] and intermediate-grade reinforcing steel (yield of 40,000 psi). The floors are constructed as a slab, beam, and girder system supported on columns, most of which are square. The column sizes vary in each story—generally from about 21 by 21 in. in the first story to 14 by 14 in. in the fifth story—but there are many exceptions. Nearly all the columns that support more than one level are spirally reinforced. The remaining columns have ties. The floor spans are relatively short by modern standards: 5.5 in. slabs span to 14 by 20 in. beams at 10 ft on center. The typical beam spans are 10 or 20 ft, with some at 15 ft. Girders measuring 14 by 26 in. span 20 ft parallel to the exterior walls and support a beam at midspan.

The roof at Ring E is gabled (as are those over Ring A and the radial corridors). Slabs 4.5 in. thick span perpendicular to the exterior wall with spans varying from about 8 to 11 ft. The slabs are supported by 12 by 16 in. purlins that span to rafter frames, which are 20 ft on center. The rafters are generally 16 by 24 in. and align with the floor beams and columns below. In general, the purlins do not align with the floor girders and columns below.

The roof over rings B, C, and D consists of a nearly flat pan joist and slab system. The joist stems are 6 in. wide by 8 in. deep and the slab is 2.75 in. thick. The joists are 26 in. on center and span 20 ft. The roof over the corridors is 4.5 in. thick and spans 10 ft. The joists and slab are supported by 14 by 20 in. girders that are in line with the floor girders.

The perimeter exterior walls of Ring E are faced in limestone and backed with unreinforced brick infilled in the concrete frame. Nearly all remaining exterior walls are 10 in. concrete. The first story at AE Drive is brick infilled in the concrete frame, with no windows. [The AE Drive refers to the light well between rings B and C, which extends to the ground over most of the building's circumference.] The concrete walls have 5 by 7 ft openings for windows and include columns built in as pilasters, corresponding to column locations below, and girders reinforced within the wall.

Slabs, beams, and girders all make use of straight and trussed bars. Except for the top reinforcement in the short spans adjacent to longer spans, there are no continuous top bars. However, approximately half of the bottom bars are made continuous by laps of 30 to 40 bar diameters at the supports. Beams and girders typically have open-topped stirrups. The longer spans generally have approximately equal areas of steel at the critical sections.

Any building is a product of its times. The Pentagon was constructed between September 1941 and January 1943. At that time the national standard predominantly used for reinforced-concrete buildings was ACI 501-36 as developed by the American Concrete Institute (ACI). Although no reference to ACI 501-36 was found in the drawings, it is very likely that this code affected decisions about member sizing and proportioning for the Pentagon structure. A brief review of some of its basic requirements is in order.

ACI 501-36 was based on working stress design. The allowable stress for the intermediate-grade billet steel used in the Pentagon was 20,000 psi. For the design concrete strength of 2,500 psi, the allowable unit shear stress for beams with properly designed web reinforcement was 150 psi. The unit bond stress for deformed bars was 125 psi for the same strength of concrete.

The estimated service load of the column was set at approximately one-third of its expected strength on the basis of the specified compressive strength of the concrete and the specified yield stress of the reinforcement.

The physical characteristics of the Pentagon structure suggest that its design may have been influenced strongly by the book *Reinforced Concrete Construction* (Hool and Pulver 1937). It is also of interest to note that this reference recommends a reinforcing arrangement similar to that for the girders. A critical attribute of the Pentagon structure was the continuity of at least half of the bottom reinforcement across the column line to lap for a distance of at least 30 bar diameters.

The columns were very important to the overall performance of the Pentagon; thus their original design was examined somewhat more closely. One of the most typical columns (type 14) apparently was designed to be economical by the original designers, because the margin of allowable capacity to demand was very close to unity in the lower stories. This computation ignores any bending moment from lateral loads, which at the time of the design were probably shown to be accommodated by the one-third increase in allowable stresses that was the fashion at the time. The live loads were reduced by 20 percent for columns supporting more than one floor, the common rule for storage loads.

Examination of the column design data leads to the conclusion that the minimum size used for columns was 14 in. square and that tied reinforcement was used until higher loads demanded a change. The first change was to spiral reinforcement, a 25 percent increase in allowable load by the standard of the day. The next change was in the size of the column. Given the nature of formwork at the time, today's imperative of keeping column sizes constant was obviously not an issue.

## 3.1 AIRCRAFT DATA

The impacting airplane was a Boeing 757-200 aircraft, originally delivered in 1991. This aircraft was designed to accommodate approximately 200 passengers and 1,670 cu ft of cargo. The wingspan, overall length, and tail height were respectively 124 ft 10 in., 155 ft 3 in., and 44 ft 6 in. Maximum takeoff weight was 255,000 lb, including up to 11,275 gal of fuel. Much of the aircraft fuel was contained in wing tanks. The aircraft was designed to cruise up to 3,900 nautical miles at a speed of Mach 0.80 (approximately 890 ft/s). The two engines were manufactured by Rolls-Royce and had 44,000 lb of combined thrust.

When the aircraft departed from Washington's Dulles International Airport on the morning of September 11, 2001, it held 64 persons—passengers and crew members—and enough fuel for the cross-country trip to Los Angeles. According to the National Transportation Safety Board, the aircraft weighed approximately 181,520 lb and was traveling at 460 knots (780 ft/s) on a magnetic bearing of 70 degrees when it struck the Pentagon. The aircraft had on board approximately 36,200 lb (5,300 gal.) of fuel at the time of impact.

According to Boeing engineers, the weight in each wing was composed of the following:

> Exposed wing structure: 13,500 lb
>
> Engine and struts: 11,900 lb
>
> Landing gear: 3,800 lb
>
> Fuel: 14,600 lb
>
> Total: 43,800 lb

The balance of the weight was in the fuselage. In the normal course of use the center fuel tank is the last filled and the first used. Thus the weight of the fuselage at the time of impact was $181,520 - (2 \times 43,800) = 93,920$ lb. Of this, $36,200 - (2 \times 14,600) = 7,000$ lb was fuel in the center tank.

## 3.7 SUMMARY OF THE IMPACT

The Boeing 757 approached the west wall of the Pentagon from the southwest at approximately 780 ft/s. As it approached the Pentagon site it was so low to the ground that it reportedly clipped an antenna on a vehicle on an adjacent road and severed light posts. When it was approximately 320 ft from the west wall of the building (0.42 seconds before impact), it was flying nearly level, only a few feet above the ground. The aircraft flew over the grassy area next to the Pentagon until its right wing struck a piece of construction equipment [a 750-kilowatt generator] that was approximately 100 to 110 ft from the face of the building (0.10 seconds before impact). At that time the aircraft had rolled slightly to the left, its right wing elevated. After the plane had traveled approximately another 75 ft, the left engine struck the ground at nearly the same instant that the nose of the aircraft struck the west wall of the Pentagon. Impact of the fuselage was at column line 14, at or slightly below the second-floor slab. The left wing passed below the second-floor slab, and the right wing crossed at a shallow angle from below the second-floor slab to above the second-floor slab.

A large fireball engulfed the exterior of the building in the impact area. Interior fires began immediately.

The impact upon the west facade removed first-floor columns from column lines 10 to 14. First-floor exterior columns on column lines 9, 15, 16, and 17 were severely damaged, perhaps to the point of losing all capacity. The second-floor exterior column on column line 14 and its adjacent spandrel beams were destroyed or seriously damaged. Additionally, there was facade damage on both sides of the impact area, including damage as high as the fourth floor. However, in the area of the impact of the fuselage and the tail, severe impact damage did not extend above the third-floor slab.

Immediately upon impact, the Ring E structure deflected downward over the region from an expansion joint on column line 11 south to the west exterior column on column line 18. The deformation was the most severe at the expansion joint, where the deflection was approximately 18 in. to 2 ft.

The structure was able to maintain this deformed shape for approximately 20 minutes, at which point all five levels of Ring E collapsed from column line 11 to approximately column line 18.

## 5. BPS SITE INSPECTIONS

Members of the BPS team inspected the site on two occasions. Between September 14 and September 21, 2001, team leader Paul Mlakar had limited access to the site while rescue and recovery operations were still in progress. On this early inspection visit, he examined the exterior of the building and portions of the building interior.

Controlled access to the site was granted to the full team after rescue and recovery operations were complete. On October 4, 2001, the Pentagon team, together with John Durrant, the executive director of ASCE's institutes, and W. Gene Corley, the BPS team leader at the World Trade Center, inspected the interior and exterior of the damaged area of the Pentagon for approximately four hours.

The teams attempted to inspect and photograph all columns with significant visible damage and most of the beams and floor bays with significant visible damage. To the extent possible, it was noted whether physical loads or the effects of fire caused the observed damage. The BPS team also noted the performance of windows and exterior wall reinforcements that had been installed to enhance blast resistance in Wedge 1 prior to the attack. However, the BPS team inspections were not comprehensive, and they did not address fire-related material degradation.

The collapsed portion of Ring E was immediately south of an expansion joint on column line 11. The collapsed area extended south from the expansion joint to approximately column line 15 on the east side of Ring E and to approximately column line 18 on the west side of Ring E. No portion of Ring D or Ring C collapsed; nor did either of the two-story sections between the rings. Since all debris was removed prior to the detailed inspection, the team was unable to determine specifically the level and extent of impact damage in this region of the building.

In general, the first-floor interior columns were severely damaged immediately adjacent to the collapse area on the north side of the expansion joint on column line 11 in Ring E. First-floor columns 11A, 11B, and 11C to the north of the expansion joint were missing. Upper columns on the north side of the expansion joint on column line 11 were intact, except for the second-floor columns at 11A and 11B. These columns were severed at the second floor, which was also damaged at this location.

None of the facade in the collapse area was accessible for inspection. However, the team did observe that limestone of the first-floor facade was seriously damaged to the north to column line 8. Some first-floor limestone panels of the facade were missing for an additional 30 to 50 ft to the north.

The first-floor exterior column on column line 9 remained in place, but the rest of the exterior columns south to column line 11, at the start of the collapsed area, were gone. To the south, facade panels on both the first and second floors between column lines 18 and 20 were severely damaged.

The exterior of the building showed clear evidence of the extensive fire that occurred within the building. The limestone facade was blackened by smoke for more than 200 ft to the north of the impact point. Evidence of fire damage was less severe to the south, and even immediately adjacent to the impact area the facade to the south showed little evidence of fire damage.

The west facade of the Pentagon was severely scarred by debris impact, particularly to the south of the collapse area. Just above the second-floor slab, the exterior columns on column lines 18 and 19 exhibited aligning gashes that seem to indicate impact by the right wing of the aircraft. An area of broken limestone of the facade over the exterior column on column line 20 also aligned with these gashes. The fire station to the north of the heliport and the impact area was also damaged by flying debris.

The team observed that the upgraded window system was generally still in place within the reinforced frames. Windows that had not been upgraded generally were broken for several hundred feet to the north of the impact point.

The aircraft had entered the building at an angle, traveling in a northeasterly direction. With the possible exception of the immediate vicinity of the fuselage's entry point at column line 14, essentially all interior impact damage was inflicted in the first story: The aircraft seems for the most part to have slipped between the first floor slab on grade and the second floor. The path of damage extended from the west exterior wall of the building in a northeasterly direction completely through Ring E, Ring D, Ring C, and their connecting lower floors. There was a hole in the east wall of Ring C, emerging into AE Drive, between column lines 5 and 7 in Wedge 2. The wall failure was approximately 310 ft from where the fuselage of the aircraft entered the west wall of the building. The path of the aircraft debris passed approximately 225 ft diagonally through Wedge 1 and approximately 85 ft diagonally through a portion of Ring C in Wedge 2.

Columns and beams along the path of the debris and within the fire area were damaged to varying degrees. Some columns and beams were missing entirely, while others nearby sometimes appeared unscathed.

Most of the serious structural damage was within a swath that was approximately 75 to 80 ft wide and extended approximately 230 ft into the first floor of the building. This swath was oriented at approximately 35 to 40 degrees to the perpendicular to the exterior wall of the Pentagon. Within the swath of serious damage was a narrower, tapering area that contained most of the very severe structural damage. This tapering area approximated a triangle in plan and had a width of approximately 90 ft at the aircraft's entry point and a length of approximately 230 ft along the trajectory of the aircraft through the building.

Severe damage included heavy cracking and spalling, either from impact or from the ensuing fire. The concrete cover had been completely dislodged from the spirally reinforced core concrete and steel of the most heavily damaged columns that remained in place.

Several columns were substantially distorted, exhibiting lateral displacement at the column midheight equal to at least three times the diameter of the spiral cage. Some highly distorted columns were bent in uniform curvature with discrete hinges at each end, while others were bent into triple curvature. In these cases, the vertical column steel remained attached to the foundation below and the second-floor beams above. The deformed shapes of the columns with this damage were smooth curves: generally, they did not have discrete deformation cusps.

In the worst cases, first-floor columns were severed from the second floor above or from the slab on grade or were missing entirely. Severed columns generally were lying on the slab on grade, still attached to the floor. These columns were straight (except for the discrete bends at the connections to the floor) in their prone positions.

## 6.1 IMPACT DAMAGE

The site data indicate that the aircraft fuselage impacted the building at column line 14 at an angle of approximately 42 degrees to the normal to the face of the building, at or slightly below the second-story slab. Eyewitness accounts and photographs taken by a security camera suggest that the aircraft was flying on nearly a level path essentially at grade level for several hundred feet immediately prior to impact. Gashes in the facade above the second-floor slab between column lines 18 and 20 to the south of the collapse area suggest that the aircraft had rolled slightly to the left as it entered the building. The right wing was below the second-floor slab at the fuselage but above the second-floor slab at the tip, and the left wing struck the building entirely below the second-floor slab, to the north of column line 14.

The width of the severe damage to the west facade of the Pentagon was approximately 120 ft (from column lines 8 to 20). The projected width, perpendicular to the path of the aircraft, was approximately 90 ft, which is substantially less than the 125 ft wingspan of the aircraft. An examination of the area encompassed by extending the line of travel of the aircraft to the face of the building shows that there are no discrete marks on the building corresponding to the positions of the outer third of the right wing. The size and position of the actual opening in the facade of the building (from column line 8 to column line 18) indicate that no portion of the outer two-thirds of the right wing and no portion of the outer one-third of the left wing actually entered the building.

It is possible that less of the right wing than the left wing entered the building because the right wing struck the facade crossing the level of the second-floor slab. The strength of the second-floor slab in its own plane would have severed the right wing approximately at the location of the right engine. The left wing did not encounter a slab, so it penetrated more easily.

In any event, the evidence suggests that the tips of both wings did not make direct contact with the facade of the building and that portions of the wings might have been separated from the fuselage before the aircraft struck the building. This is consistent with eyewitness statements that the right wing struck a large generator before the aircraft struck the building and that the left engine struck a ground-level, external vent structure. It is possible that these impacts, which occurred not more than 100 ft before the nose of the aircraft struck the building, may have damaged the wings and caused debris to strike the Pentagon facade and the heliport control building.

The wing fuel tanks are located primarily within the inner half of the wings. The center of gravity of these tanks is approximately one-third of the wing length from the fuselage. Considering this tank position and the physical evidence of the length of each wing that could not have entered the building, it appears likely that not more than half of the fuel in the right wing could have entered the building. While the full volume of the left wing tank was within the portion of the wing that might have entered the building, some of the fuel from all tanks rebounded upon impact and contributed to the fireball. Only a portion of the fuel from the left and right wing tanks and the center fuselage tank actually entered the building.

The height of the damage to the facade of the building was much less than the height of the aircraft's tail. At approximately 45 ft., the tail height was nearly as tall as the first four floors of the building. Obvious visible damage extended only over the lowest two floors, to approximately 25 ft above grade.

In formulating opinions about columns in the collapse area, the BPS team interpreted photographs taken after impact and before collapse. The team members do not have direct information on the impact damage to the upper floors in the collapsed portion of the building. However, based on observations of the condition of the adjoining structure and the photographs of the building before the collapse, the following general observations may be made:

Impact damage on the first floor was extensive near the entry point of the aircraft. It is likely that the exterior first-floor columns from column line 10 to column line 14 were removed entirely by the impact and that the exterior columns on column lines 9, 15, 16, and 17 were severely damaged. Most probably, many or most of the first-floor interior columns in the collapse area were heavily damaged by impact.

The removal of the second-floor exterior column on column line 14, probably by the fuselage tail, suggests that the second-floor slab in this area was also severely damaged even before the building collapsed. In the portion of the building that remained standing to the north of the expansion joint, the slab and second-floor columns at column lines A, B, and C were heavily damaged. This condition, which is consistent with the trajectory of the aircraft, suggests that the second-floor slab from the expansion joint on column line 11 south to the fuselage entry point on column line 14—including columns 11B, 11C, and 13A on the second floor—was heavily damaged, perhaps destroyed.

It is difficult to judge the condition of other columns on the second floor in the collapse area. However, more likely than not column 15A was relatively undamaged. It is unlikely that columns above the second floor sustained impact damage, even in the area that ultimately collapsed.

Impact damage to the structure above the second-floor slab did not extend more than approximately 50 ft into the building. This shows that the aircraft slid between the first-floor slab on grade and the second-floor slab for most of its distance of travel after striking the building.

Along the path of the movement of aircraft debris through the building, the most severe damage was confined to a region that can be represented approximately by a triangle centered on the trajectory of the aircraft in plan, with a base width at the aircraft entry point of approximately 90 ft and a length along the aircraft path of approximately 230 ft. However, within this triangular damage area there were a few relatively lightly damaged columns interspersed with heavily damaged columns along the path of the aircraft debris through the building. Column 1K, located 200 ft from the impact point, was the last severed column along the path of the aircraft. Note that columns on grids E and K are much weaker than the other columns because they support only one floor and a roof.

There were two areas of severe impact damage in the first story. The first area along the path of the aircraft was within approximately 60 ft of the impact point and corresponds generally to the area that collapsed. In the collapse area and for approximately 20 ft beyond the collapse area along its northern and eastern edges, columns were removed or very severely damaged by impact. In addition, there was serious second-floor beam and slab damage for 60 ft to the north of the collapse area, especially along a strip bounded approximately by column lines B and C.

The second area of severe damage was bounded approximately by column lines E, 5, G, and 9. In this region, which was beyond a field of columns that remained standing, several columns were severed and there was significant second-floor beam and slab damage. In both areas, severe slab damage appeared to be caused by moving debris rather than by overpressure from a blast. In an effort to characterize the influence of the aircraft on the structure and, by extension, to characterize the loads on the structure, the team analyzed the available data to extract information about the destruction of the aircraft.

Most likely, the wings of the aircraft were severed as the aircraft penetrated the facade of the building. Even if portions of the wings remained intact after passing through the plane of the facade, the structural damage pattern indicates that the wings were severed before the aircraft penetrated more than a few dozen feet into the building. Ultimately, the path of the fuselage debris passed between columns 9C and 11D, which were separated by approximately 28 ft at a depth of approximately 65 ft along the aircraft's path. Columns 9C and 11D were severely distorted but still in place: Hence, the wings clearly did not survive beyond this point.

At a depth of approximately 160 ft into the building, columns 3G, 3H, 3J, and 5J were damaged but still standing, although in the direct path of the fuselage. With a maximum spacing of less than 14 ft between pairs of these columns in a projection perpendicular to the path of the fuselage, it is highly unlikely that any significant portion of the fuselage could have retained structural integrity at this point in its travel. More likely, the fuselage was destroyed much earlier in its movement through the building. Therefore, the aircraft frame most certainly was destroyed before it had traveled a distance that approximately equaled the length of the aircraft.

The debris that traveled the farthest traveled approximately twice the length of the aircraft after entering the building. To come to rest at a point 310 ft from the area of impact at a speed of 780 ft/s, that debris experienced an average deceleration of approximately 30 $g$'s.

The influence of the structure on the deceleration of the aircraft (and, conversely, the influence of the aircraft on the structure) can be appreciated by comparisons with examples of aircraft belly-landed in controlled circumstances. In 1984, the Federal Aviation Administration (FAA) conducted a controlled impact demonstration (Department of Transportation 1987) to evaluate the burn potential of antimisting kerosene fuel. In that test, the FAA landed a Boeing 720 aircraft (weighing approximately 175,000 lb) without landing gear on a gravel runway at Edwards Air Force Base. The aircraft in that test was flying at approximately 250 ft/s when it made first contact, but it slid approximately 1,200 ft before it stopped. Although the test aircraft was traveling at approximately one-third the speed of the aircraft that struck the Pentagon, its sliding distance was approximately 3.9 times that of the Pentagon attack aircraft. Clearly, the short stopping distance for the aircraft striking the Pentagon derived from the energy dissipated through the destruction of the aircraft and building components; the acceleration of building contents; the loss of lift when the wings were severed from the aircraft; and effective frictional and impact forces on the first-floor slab, the underside of the second-floor slab, and interior columns and walls.

A study of the locations of fatalities also yields insight into the breakup of the aircraft and, therefore, its influence on the structure. The remains of most of the passengers on the aircraft were found near the end of the travel of the aircraft debris. The front landing gear (a relatively solid and heavy object) and the flight data recorder (which had been located near the rear of the aircraft) were also found nearly 300 ft into the structure. By contrast, the remains of a few individuals (the hijacking suspects), who most likely were near the front of the aircraft, were found relatively close to the aircraft's point of impact with the building. These data suggest that the front of the aircraft disintegrated essentially upon impact but, in the process, opened up a hole allowing the trailing portions of the fuselage to pass into the building.

Several columns exhibited severe bends. However, the predominant evidence suggests that these columns generally did not receive impact from a single, rigid object. Instead, the deformed shapes of these columns are more consistent with loads that were distributed over the height of the columns.

The analyses of the available data reveal that the wings severed exterior columns but were not strong enough to cut through the second-floor slab upon impact. (The right wing did not enter the building at the point where it struck the second-floor slab in its plane.) The damage pattern throughout the building and the locations of fatalities and aircraft components, together with the deformation of columns, suggest that the entire aircraft disintegrated rapidly as it moved through the forest of columns on the first floor. As the moving debris from the aircraft pushed the contents and demolished exterior wall of the building forward, the debris from the aircraft and building most likely resembled a rapidly moving avalanche through the first floor of the building.

## 6.3 EXTERIOR WALL UPGRADES

The structural upgrades of the exterior wall performed reasonably well, considering that they were not specifically designed for aircraft impact. The only window frames removed by the impact were those struck directly by the wings or the fuselage. On the second floor, immediately adjacent to where the fuselage entered the building, upgraded windows remained in their frames even though the surrounding masonry facade was completely removed.

Upgraded glass was generally not broken immediately after the impact or after the ensuing fire had been extinguished. By contrast, most of the original windows in a vast area of Wedge 2 were broken after the fire was extinguished. It is probable that some of these windows were broken by the fire or by fire-fighting efforts rather than by the effects of the impact.

## 7.1 RESPONSE OF COLUMNS TO IMPACT

The structural elements of the Pentagon that bore the brunt of the airplane impact were the first-story columns. All columns in the first story had square cross sections and spirally reinforced cores with a concrete cover of $1\frac{1}{2}$ in.

The story height was 14 ft 1 in. There were two different arrangements of longitudinal reinforcement. The side dimensions varied from approximately 1 ft to 2 ft. Longitudinal reinforcement ratios ranged from approximately 1.5 to 2.5 percent. The minimum spiral reinforcement ratio was 1.3 percent.

Moment-curvature relationships for these columns were calculated assuming a mean concrete cylinder strength of 4,000 psi and a yield stress in the longitudinal reinforcement of 45,000 psi. The spirally reinforced concrete core had a considerably higher calculated limiting unit curvature capacity than that calculated for the gross section of the column treated as a "tied column." The spiral cores possessed two other important properties not evident in those plots that define only cross-sectional response:

1) The cores enclosed by spiral reinforcement had shear strength higher than the shear corresponding to that associated with the development of the flexural strength of the core under lateral loading. For the limiting static uniform load corresponding to the critical failure mechanism, the maximum unit shear stress did not exceed three-fourths of the estimated unit shear strength of the core.

2) The longitudinal bars had sufficient anchorage to develop their strengths.

These two properties eliminated the possibility of brittle failure of the cores. Indeed, none of the columns was observed to have failed in shear, and there was no evidence of pull-out of reinforcing bars. The cores and their connections did not unravel under impact. Destroying the column core required tearing it off its supports. The longitudinal reinforcing bars at ends of the severely damaged columns were observed to have fractured after necking, indicating ductile failure.

The plot describing the response of the gross section of the columns (tied columns) refers to a section subjected to flexure with the shell concrete intact and assuming that the shear stresses would not precipitate failure. Had the columns been tied columns—that is, columns without spiral reinforcement confining the core—even the modest unit-curvature limits shown in the figures would not have been attained because shear failure would have preceded development of the yield moments at the critical sections.

The impact effects may be represented as a violent flow through the structure of a "fluid" consisting of aviation fuel and solid fragments. The first-story columns in the path of this rushing fluid mass must have lost their shells immediately on impact. The curves with the higher moment capacities are, in effect, irrelevant for the affected columns. It is very likely that there was never a finite time in which the affected columns responded as tied columns. The column shells must have been scoured off on first contact with the fluid.

Bending resistance to the pressure created by the velocity of the fluid must have occurred in the cores only. The limits of the moment-curvature relationships for the column cores shown were based on a nominal fracture strain of 0.2 in the reinforcement in tension.

Several numerical simulations of a fluid mass (in this case modeled as aviation fuel) impacting a reinforced-concrete column fixed top and bottom were made by S.A. Kilic in support of the BPS team. These simulations indicated that the maximum response velocity of the column was comparable to the velocity of the impacting fluid. The conclusion for the facade columns is self-evident. Their maximum response velocities could not have been less than 600 ft/s (vis-à-vis the impact velocity of approximately 780 ft/s). These columns engulfed by the fluid would have been destroyed immediately, however much energy might have been deflected by the facade walls and slabs. The question of interest is whether there was any system to the distribution of the severely damaged columns in the first story.

It is plausible to expect that the energy content of the impacting fluid mass attenuated—as it penetrated the building—as the square of the distance from the point of impact. Recognizing that the debris was not thrown more than a distance of 310 ft and accepting the impact velocity of approximately 780 ft/s, it may be inferred that the velocity of the fluid would have reached a value of approximately 100 ft/s, a velocity that, at a distance approaching 200 ft from the point of impact, most column cores would be expected to resist without disintegration.

There is no question that the progress of the impacting fluid in the structure must have verged on the chaotic. The reasoning in the preceding paragraphs is not presented as a prediction of an orderly process but as a preliminary rationalization of the distribution of severe damage to the spirally reinforced column cores immediately after impact. The important conclusion is that the observed distribution of failed columns does not contradict simple estimates made on the basis of elementary mechanics. There is promise in further analyses of the phenomena observed. The same reasoning would suggest that had the columns in the affected region been tied columns, all would have been destroyed, leading to immediate collapse of a large portion of the building.

A frame from a physics-based simulation of an idealized airplane loaded with fuel impacting a set of spirally reinforced concrete columns (by Hoffmann and Kilic of Purdue University) senses the deceleration of the airframe as indicated by the buckling of the fuselage. It is also interesting to note that the columns are shown to tear into the airframe but get destroyed by the mass of the fluid in the wing tanks, events confirmed by the distribution of the debris.

The necking of the reinforcing bars is evidence of the proper performance of the bar anchorages. If energy absorption is a design objective, the evidence suggests that spirally reinforced concrete columns are the right choice.

## 7.3 THERMAL RESPONSE OF COLUMNS AND GIRDERS

Prior to the collapse of portions of the structural system in Wedge 1 of Ring E, which occurred approximately 20 minutes after the impact of the aircraft, the fire that was first ignited by the ejected jet A fuel had transitioned from the growth stage and become a ventilation-controlled "fully developed" or "postflashover" fire. In a ventilation-controlled postflashover fire, the flames typically project from windows and openings because there is insufficient air in the burning rooms to allow all the combustible gases to burn within the rooms.

Estimation of the fire intensity—that is, maximum temperatures and time-temperature characteristics—of postflashover fires is important in understanding the effect of fire on exposed structural elements. However, the accuracy of such estimation depends on a correct estimation of the fire fuel load (hydrocarbon-based building and aircraft contents and jet A fuel) and the ventilation factor. This cannot be done with a high degree of exactness even in a typical building fire. In the case of the Pentagon attack, it is further complicated by the lack of complete knowledge of the available fuel load (besides the ejected jet A fuel) and by the unconventional ventilation factor.

### 7.3.1. LOADING

The fire intensity can be estimated if the fire fuel load [is] known. The maximum fuel capacity listed for the Boeing 757-200 is 11,275 gal (www.boeing.com). According to information provided by the National Transportation Safety Board, the aircraft had on board about 5,300 gal of jet A fuel, or approximately 36,200 lb of fuel based on the density of 6.8 lb/gal, at the time of impact. Based on images captured by the Pentagon security camera, which showed the aircraft approaching and the subsequent explosion and fireball, it is estimated that about 4,900 lb of jet fuel was involved in the prompt fire and was consumed at the time of impact outside the building. This leaves about 30,400 lb as the estimated mass of the jet fuel that entered the building and contributed to the fire fuel load within the building.

The net calorific value or heat of combustion—that is, the amount of heat released during complete combustion of a unit mass of fuel—measured for jet fuel is 18,916.6 Btu/lb. Thus, the maximum possible energy that could have been released inside the building by the complete burning of 30,400 lb of jet A fuel is 575,064,488 Btu.

It is assumed that the fuel was initially contained within the first floor, in a "room" bounded by the path of damage caused by the impact of the airplane. The estimated total surface area (floor, ceiling, and bounding walls including windows and openings) of the room is about 36,597 sq ft. The fire fuel load contributed by the available jet A fuel alone can be computed as 15,713 Btu/sq ft.

As indicated, within the first half an hour of the aircraft impact, the fire had become fully developed within some compartments of the Pentagon. This means combustible building and aircraft contents had begun to burn and therefore contributed to the fire fuel load. The exact fire fuel load contributed by the building and aircraft contents is not known because of insufficient information on the type of occupancy in this particular section of the Pentagon. However, a lower-bound estimate can be made using data recommended by the International Council for Research and Innovation in Building and Construction, or CIB, which lists average fuel loads for different types of building occupancy (International Council, 1986).

It is assumed that the type of occupancy of the Pentagon is such that the fire fuel load of its building and aircraft contents is equivalent to the lowest value of the four CIB office types of occupancy; since the CIB-recommended fuel loads are for design purposes, it is believed that they include the safety factor, the magnitude of which is unfortunately not known. Thus, a conservative safety factor of 2 can be assumed in the CIB recommendation. The lower bound of the fire fuel load contributed by the building and aircraft contents can then be estimated to be about 17,611 Btu/sq ft. The combined total fire fuel load can then be estimated to be about 33,325 Btu/sq ft.

The room opening in this case is estimated to be about 75 percent of the total area of the building elevation along column line AA that is limited to the first story and bounded between column lines 8 and 19. The 75 percent area accounted for the existing windows and the opening created by the impact of the airplane. The total surface area in the first story between column lines 8 and 19 is about 1,098 sq ft based on a height of 10 ft. The time-temperature curves for different fuel loads and ventilation factors, produced by Magnusson and Thelandersson (1970), are widely used for estimating real fire exposure.

It should be noted that the estimated time-temperature curves for all fire fuel loads in this figure have the same initial rate of temperature rise (the first 10 minutes of the fire), and this initial rate of temperature rise is higher than that prescribed for standard fire ASTM [American Society for Testing Materials] E-119 but lower than that of standard hydrocarbon pool fire ASTM E-1529. Similarly, within the first half-hour of the fire (prior to collapse) the temperature of the estimated fire was slightly higher than the ASTM E-119 temperature but lower than the temperature prescribed by ASTM E-1529.

## 8. FINDINGS

Through observations at the crash site and approximate analyses, the team determined that the direct impact of the aircraft destroyed the load capacity of about 30 first-floor columns and significantly impaired that of about 20 others along a diagonal path that extended along a swath that was approximately 75 ft wide by 230 ft long through the first floor. This impact may also have destroyed the load capacity of about six second-floor columns adjacent to the exterior wall. While the impact scoured the cover of around 30 other columns, their spiral reinforcement conspicuously preserved some of their load capacity. The impact further destroyed the load capacity of the second-floor system adjoining the exterior wall.

The subsequent fire fed by the aircraft fuel, the aircraft contents, and the building contents caused damage throughout a very large area of the first story, a significant area of the second, a small part of the third, and only in the stairwells above. This fire caused serious spalling of the reinforced-concrete frame only in a few, small, isolated areas on the first and second stories. Subsequent petrographic examination showed more widespread heat damage to the concrete.

Despite the extensive column damage on the first floor, the collapse of the floors above was extremely limited. Frame and yield-line analyses attribute this life-saving response to the following factors:

- Redundant and alternative load paths of the beam and girder framing system;
- Short spans between columns;
- Substantial continuity of beam and girder bottom reinforcement through the supports;
- Design for 150 psf [pounds per square foot] warehouse live load in excess of service load;

- Significant residual load capacity of damaged spirally reinforced columns;
- Ability of the exterior walls to act as transfer girders.

An area covering approximately 50 by 60 ft of the upper floors above the point of impact did collapse approximately 20 minutes after the impact. Thermal analyses indicate that the deleterious effect of the fire on the structural frame, together with impact damage that removed protective materials and compromised strength initially, was the likely cause of the limited collapse in this region.

# NOTES

## Chapter 1: The Planes

### INTRODUCTION

Information on the number of passengers in the hijacked planes: *The 9/11 Commission Report.*

### THE HIJACKERS' FLYING SKILLS

Most difficult elements of flying: interview with Brian Marsh, flight instructor, Florida-based Airline Transport Professionals Flight School, April 25, 2006; interview with Alison Duquette, spokeswoman, Federal Aviation Administration (FAA), April 27, 2006.

Hijackers' flight training: *The 9/11 Commission Report.*

FAA requirements for pilot training: Alison Duquette, FAA; U.S. Department of Labor *Occupational Outlook Handbook*; *Federal Aviation Regulations/Aeronautical Information Manual.*

Hijackers' purchases of GPS units; hijackers' whereabouts directly preceding September 11, 2001: *The 9/11 Commission Report*; "Source: Records suggest Atta in NYC on Sept. 10," CNN.com, May 22, 2002.

Hanjour's use of autopilot on Flight 77: *The 9/11 Commission Report.*

Hijackers' errant flying: *The 9/11 Commission Report.*

Estimates on how far away the WTC and the Pentagon could be seen on September 11, 2001: interview with Brian Marsh, Airline Transport Professionals Flight School, April 25, 2006.

Flight attendant Madeline Sweeney's comments on Flight 11: *The 9/11 Commission Report.*

## WHERE'S THE POD?

The possibility of retrofitting a passenger jet with undercarriage missiles: e-mail to *Popular Mechanics* from Skip Aldous, retired Air Force squadron commander, December 20, 2004.

## FLIGHT 175'S WINDOWS

Flight 175's flight path on its approach to Manhattan: *Final Report of the National Construction Safety Team on the Collapses of the World Trade Center.*

## NO STAND-DOWN ORDER

Number of fighters on alert on September 11, 2001: interview with Major Douglas Martin, former spokesman, NORAD, December 10, 2004.

Lack of computer network or alarm system to alert NORAD of hijackings: interview with Major Darren G. Steele, public affairs officer, NORAD, May 9, 2006.

Flight-intercept protocol in place on September 11, 2001: interview with Major Douglas Martin, NORAD, December 10, 2004; interview with Laura Brown, spokeswoman, FAA, May 16, 2006; Joint Chiefs of Staff instruction paper, Aircraft Piracy (Hijacking) and Destruction of Derelict Airborne Objects, June 2001; FAA regulations, Order 7610,4J, "Special Military Operations."

Methods of tracking planes: multiple interviews with Laura Brown, FAA, December 2004 and May 2006.

Information on hijackers turning off transponders: interview with Bill Schuman, public affairs officer, FAA, November 29, 2004; interview with Major Douglas Martin, NORAD, December 10, 2004.

Number of radar signals nationally; number of radar signals per air traffic controller: interviews with Laura Brown, FAA, December 2004 and May 2006; interviews with Hank Price, public affairs officer, FAA, December 2004; interviews with Ted Lopatkiewicz, public affairs officer, National Transportation Safety Board, December 2004.

Standard scramble procedure in place on September 11, 2001, for Otis Air Force Base; takeoff time for the Otis F-15s; and the request to set up air patrol over New York City: interview with Major Douglas Martin, NORAD, December 10, 2004; interview with Master Sergeant David E. Somdahl, spokesman, Air National Guard, December 29, 2004; interview with Chris Yates, aviation security editor and analyst, *Jane's Defence Weekly*, London.

Langley scramble procedures: interview with Staff Sergeant Sean McEntee, public affairs specialist, 113th Wing of the District of Columbia Air National Guard, April 27, 2006.

Dulles air controllers alert to the Secret Service: *The 9/11 Commission Report*.

"Breaking windows" quote: *The 9/11 Commission Report*.

Information on hijacker's transmission to Cleveland Center and the delayed request for military assistance: *The 9/11 Commission Report*.

Confirmation of President Bush's shoot-down order: *The 9/11 Commission Report*.

Unprecedented type of hijacking: Chris Yates, *Jane's Defence Weekly*. There are two other known incidents in which the hijackers' stated mission was to fly a plane into a building. According to a spokesman at the Baltimore/Washington International Airport, Samuel Byck stormed a Delta plane in 1974 while it was at the gate prior to a flight to Atlanta. Byck's stated intention was to fly the aircraft into the White House in order to assassinate President Richard M. Nixon. In the ensuing shoot-out, police wounded Byck, who then shot and killed himself. In 1994, according to *Jane's Defence Weekly*, four members of the Armed Islamic Group commandeered an Air France plane in Algiers with the intention to fly it to Paris and crash into the Eiffel Tower. The pilots flew the plane to Marseilles, where French commandos stormed the aircraft and killed the hijackers.

## MILITARY INTERCEPTS

Information on Payne Stewart's Learjet and the intercept by the F-16 from Eglin Air Force Base: Aircraft Accident Brief DCA00MA005, National Transportation and Safety Board, October 25, 1999. An article in *Sports Illustrated* (April 10, 2000) reports that two National Guard F-16s from Tyndall Air Force Base in Panama City, Florida, scrambled and briefly pursued Payne's Learjet before returning to base. Officials at Tyndall tell *Popular Mechanics* that they have no record of such a scramble.

Information on the ADIZ: The FAA's *Aeronautical Information Manual: Official Guide to Basic Flight Information and ATC Procedures*.

Information on NORAD interceptions from the end of the Cold War until September 11, 2001, and the increased interagency cooperation since then: interview with Major Darren G. Steele, NORAD, May 9, 2006.

Warren Rudman quote: *Boston Globe*, September 15, 2001.

# Chapter 2: World Trade Center Towers 1 & 2

## INTRODUCTION

The 1945 Empire State Building aviation accident: article by William Roberts in *Elevator World*, March 1996, reprinted on the Web site www. empirestatebuilding.com; *Why Buildings Fall Down: How Structures Fail*, by Matthys Levy and Mario Salvadori, 1994.

Public statement of Texas A&M president Robert Gates regarding Morgan Reynolds, issued June 15, 2005.

## THE EMPIRE STATE BUILDING ACCIDENT

Skyscraper construction methods: "The Tower Builder," an article by John Seabrook in the November 19, 2001, issue of the *New Yorker*, is an excellent overview of evolving twentieth-century skyscraper construction methods, including the design and engineering of the WTC towers.

## WIDESPREAD DAMAGE

The Federal Emergency Management Agency (FEMA) preliminary report— *World Trade Center Building Performance Study: Data Collection, Preliminary Observations and Recommendations*—had a budget of $600,000 and was released in May 2002, nine months after the attacks. The National Institute of Standards and Technology (NIST) report, titled *Final Report on the Collapse of the World Trade Center Towers,* was budgeted at $24 million and took three years to prepare. It was released in September 2005.

World Trade Center environs and building damages on September 11: NIST report; *Baseline Structural Performance and Aircraft Impact Damage Analysis of the World Trade Center Towers*, NIST supplement report, September 2005.

Overall building performance and lobby damage: interviews with Shyam Sunder, deputy director of the building and fire research laboratory at NIST, lead investigator, NIST report, May 2006.

Damage to tower elevators: interviews with James G. Quintiere, professor of fire protection engineering, University of Maryland, December 2004.

## MELTED STEEL

Amounts of fuel in the hijacked planes: NIST report.

Temperature at which jet fuel burns: interview with Shyam Sunder, June 7, 2006. According to Sunder, scientists measure the gradual rise of temperature in building fires according to the time-temperature relationship, measured every 10 minutes. Jet fuel fires are hydrocarbon fires, which quickly rise in temperature in a matter of several minutes to a plateau of 1,100 to 1,200 degrees Celsius (2,012 to 2,190 degrees Fahrenheit). This is the gas temperature, which is measured just next to the flame, as opposed to the flame temperature.

Difference between Twin Towers fires and other high-rise fires: NIST report.

Impact floors in Twin Towers: NIST report.

## FREE-FALL TIMES

How fast the towers fell: *Inferno at the World Trade Center,* by Eduardo Kausel, professor of civil and environmental engineering at the Massachusetts Institute of Technology (MIT). NIST report.

Analyzing news footage: NIST clarifies, "From video evidence, significant portions of the cores of both buildings (roughly 60 stories of WTC 1 and 40 stories of WTC 2) are known to have stood 15 to 25 seconds after collapse initiation before they, too, began to collapse." Collapse-time estimates are, however, close to would-be free-fall results, as shown in *Why Did the World Trade Center Collapse? Science, Engineering, and Speculation,* by Thomas Eager, the Thomas Lord Professor of Materials Engineering and Engineering Systems (MIT)

Why the towers collapsed: Keith Seffen, a senior lecturer in the engineering department at the University of Cambridge, discusses the collapse in his paper "Discussion of Progressive Collapse of the World Trade Center: A Simple Analysis."

## PUFFS OF DUST

Thickness of columns at the base of the WTC towers: NIST report.

Steven E. Jones's primary field of study: Brigham Young University (BYU) Web site.

Structural strength and behavior of steel frames under high temperatures: interview with Shyam Sunder, May 15, 2006; interview with Zdenek Bazant, McCormick School Professor and Walter P. Murphy Professor, Department of Civil and Environmental Engineering, Northwestern University, May 5, 2006; "Why Did the World Trade Center Collapse?— Simple Analysis," Zdenek Bazant, *Journal of Engineering Mechanics,* January 2002. Bazant informed *Popular Mechanics* via email that he is updating the paper, "not to try to debunk all of this nonsense but to provide a detailed mathematical description of this progressive collapse in a refereed journal of high standards addressing only those that are qualified."

BYU engineering department's assessment of Jones's online paper: *Fulton College Response to Professor Steven Jones's Statements Regarding Collapse of World Trade Center,* Ira A. Fulton, BYU's College of Engineering and Technology Web site. The report is no longer posted online.

Tests conducted by NIST: Some 200 technical experts interviewed more than 1,000 people, reviewed 7,000 segments of video footage and 7,000 photographs, analyzed 236 pieces of steel from the wreckage, and performed laboratory tests and sophisticated computer simulations of the sequence of events that occurred from the moment the aircraft struck the towers until they began to collapse. Based on this comprehensive investigation, NIST's conclusions included that World Trade Center towers collapsed because the impact of the planes severed and damaged support columns, dislodged fireproofing insulation coating the steel floor trusses and steel columns, and widely dispersed jet fuel over multiple floors.

The pancake theory of collapse: Kevin Ryan writes in the *Journal of 911 Studies* that NIST's denial of the pancake theory is in direct contradiction to the comments of Shyam Sunder, NIST's Building and Fire Research Laboratory director, reported by *Popular Mechanics* in March 2005. In that article, Sunder said that "puffs of dust" occur when a significant portion of a floor is collapsing. While the clouds of dust may create the impression of a controlled demolition, in actuality, it is the result of the floors pancaking. NIST *does* support some aspects of the theory—but does not agree that it was the trigger for the collapses. NIST report (NCSTAR 1-3) states that the overloading of the lower floors (the "pancaking" mechanism) likely did occur during the collapse of the buildings, but that it did not cause the collapse.

## "NANO-THERMITE" IN THE TOWERS

High temperatures causing collapse: NIST report.

Source of molten material: NIST report (NCSTAR 1-5A) lists the source of the molten material as aluminum alloys from the aircraft.

Thermite required to heat a pound of steel: In NIST report *(NIST-NCSTAR 1)*, researchers estimated that at least 0.13 pounds of thermite would be required to heat each pound of a steel section to approximately 700 degrees Celsius (the temperature at which steel weakens substantially).

Scientific review peer journals: *The Open Chemical Physics Journal,* one of over 250 peer-reviewed open-access journals, published by Bentham Science, charges the authors a few hundred dollars to publish their work. Researchers have found Bentham's peer-review process highly suspect. In January 2009, Philip Davis, a PhD student at Cornell University, and Kent Anderson of the New England Journal of Medicine, tested the peer-review process at the *Open Information Science Journal* by submitting a bogus article, which was accepted. The two wrote about the incident in *The Scholarly Kitchen.*

## SEISMIC SPIKES

Weight of jet fuel in the hijacked planes: NIST report.

Seismic strength of 1993 WTC truck bombing: *Seismic Waves Generated by Aircraft Impacts and Building Collapses at World Trade Center, New York City,* Won-Young Kim et al., Lamont-Doherty Earth Observatory of Columbia University, November 2001.

Seismic strength to damage buildings: U.S. Geologic Survey; University of California Lawrence Livermore National Laboratory.

Amount of time for towers to collapse: NIST report.

Oklahoma City bombing: "Seismograms Offer Insight into Oklahoma City Bombing," *American Geophysical Union,* October 8, 1996.

# Chapter 3: World Trade Center Building 7

## INTRODUCTION

The "smoking gun": Architect Gregg Roberts and David Chandler, a physics teacher, discuss how they think the NIST covered up certain facts in *Building 7 Implosion: The Smoking Gun of 9/11.*

High-profile tenants: According the news agencies such as CNN and the *New York Times,* WTC 7 housed the Secret Service, Central Intelligence Agency, Department of Defense, and Internal Revenue Service.

FEMA study: Building performance study *(World Trade Center Building Performance Study)* was released eight months after 9/11 that focused on long-burning fires as the cause of collapse. World Trade Center 7 housed five storage tanks containing some 42,000 gallons of diesel fuel that could power fourteen backup generators located throughout the building.

Three years to investigate WTC 7: The extensive three-year scientific and technical building- and fire-safety investigation found that the fires on multiple floors in WTC 7, which were uncontrolled but otherwise similar to fires experienced in other tall buildings, caused an extraordinary event, according to NIST's *Final WTC 7 Investigation Report*, released in November 2008 by the government agency. The heating of floor beams and girders caused a critical support column to fail, initiating a fire-induced progressive collapse that brought the building down.

## FIRE AND DEBRIS DAMAGE

Tenants of WTC 7: FEMA report.

New York Police Department photograph of south face of WTC 7: It was taken from an NYPD helicopter before WTC 7 collapsed and is included in the NIST report on page L-20. It clearly shows that debris from WTC 1's collapse scooped out a huge chunk of the southwest corner of the building. See NIST report, Appendix L, Figure L-22A.

Other contributing factors to WTC 7's collapse, including fuel tanks and generators: interviews with Shyam Sunder, May 2006.

Fire's role in WTC 7 collapse: NIST's initial finding in the *Progress Report on the Federal Building and Fire Safety Investigation of the World Trade Center; FEMA's World Trade Center Building Performance Study*.

WTC 7's windowless fifth floor: interviews with Shyam Sunder, May 2006.

Surfaces bursting into flames: Flashover process described by Working Fire Web site.

Fire on lower floors: On floors 7 through 9, the initial fires spread by flame contact, according to the NIST report (NCSTAR-1A). On floors 11 through 13, the flashover would have occurred in several minutes. After about 15 minutes, the ceiling tile system would likely fail and the hot gases would create a local hot upper layer. Thermal radiation from this layer would have ignited adjacent offices. Offices across a corridor would likely have ignited more slowly. The collapse of WTC 7 was not caused by diesel fuel fires or by fire-induced failure of the transfer trusses on floors 5 and 6. Instead, the fires grew from one workstation to another.

Thermal expansion contributes to the building's failure: Interview with Dr. Shyam Sunder, June 2010; *The Raw Story;* NIST report.

## WRECKAGE PILE

Exhaustive computer simulations: SHAMRC, a software program that is employed for the analysis of explosive detonations, shock propagation, and structure loads due to blast and fragments, was used to simulate pressure histories from hypothetical blasts, according to a NIST report. SHAMRC has a proven record of accuracy for explosive weights of less than 500 g (1 lb) to more than 4 x 106 kg (4,000 tons).

SHAMRC computer simulations: NIST report states that simulations were performed for differing degrees of partitioning of a tenant floor. Attention focused on a single hypothetical blast scenario. This scenario involved preliminary cutting of Column 79 and the use of 4 kg (9 lb) of RDX explosives in linear shaped charges. The other scenarios would have required more explosives, or were considered infeasible to accomplish without detection. Calculations were also performed for a lesser charge size of 1 kg (2 lb) to evaluate threshold explosive requirements for window fragility.

The empty space of WTC 7: Interview with Brent L. Blanchard, who currently serves as operations manager for Protec Documentation Services Inc., in Rancocas Woods, New Jersey, and who is the senior writer for implosionworld.com, June 2010; *Seattle Times* interview with Thomas Eager, professor of materials science at MIT.

Damage to Verizon building: *New York Times* article.

## SILVERSTEIN'S "PULL IT" QUOTE

Demolition and engineering experts on the phrase "pull it": Interviews with Jon Magnusson, CEO of Magnusson Klemencic Associates; Ron Dokell, retired president of Olshan Demolishing Company; Mark Loizeaux, president of Controlled Demolition, Inc,; and James Quintiere, Ph.D. (in mechanical engineering), professor of fire protection engineering, University of Maryland, May 2006.

Clean up efforts: Interview with Brent Blanchard from Protec Documentation Services, which was hired to photograph the cleanup efforts at Ground Zero in 2001, June 2010.

NIST and what they did not find: After an exhaustive three-year study on the collapse of WTC 7, Shyam Sunder, NIST's lead investigator, held a press conference in August 2008. "I'd like to tell you what we did not find. We did not find any evidence that explosives were used to bring the building down."

## THE DEATH OF BARRY JENNINGS

Barry Jennings Jr.: Barry Jr. writes in the "We Change the World" blog and chat room about how he spent his nineteenth birthday at Stony Brook University Hospital, watching over his father. Barry Sr. lost his battle with leukemia the next day. In the same chat room, Barry Jr. explains how his father's twin brother died from the same disease.

Confirmation of Barry Sr.'s death: Former NYC Housing Authority spokesman Howard Marder, officially confirmed that Barry Jennings (emergency coordinator and 9/11 witness) passed away after several days in the hospital, matching confirmations from several other employees at the Housing Authority.

Barry Jr.'s fiancé: Dominique Austin, speaks up in the online forum topix. com, writing that the government didn't kill Jennings Sr. over what he said in interviews of explosions inside WTC 7 before the building's collapse.

The family home in Long Island: According to real estate records obtained by *Popular Mechanics*, the Jennings's house in Long Island was foreclosed upon in 2009. According to records, as of March 2006, the bank was trying secure $320,000 and interest. According to the Austin interview, Barry Jr. lives with her in Riverhead, Long Island, and the mother lives in South Carolina.

## MINIMAL WRECKAGE TO STUDY

Truckload of debris: When the clean-up was finished, in May 2002, the workers had moved 108,000 truckloads of debris—around 1.8 million tons of material, according to How Stuff Works.

Steel used in WTC construction: The Port Authority estimates more than 200,000 tons of steel was used in the World Trade Center's construction. Of that total, more than 168,000 tons has been salvaged from Ground Zero thus far, according to the New York City Office of Emergency Management.

The experts needed: Some 200 technical experts—including about 85 career NIST experts and 125 leading experts from the private sector and academia—reviewed tens of thousands of documents, interviewed more than 1,000 people, reviewed 7,000 segments of video footage and 7,000 photographs, analyzed 236 pieces of steel from the wreckage, performed laboratory tests and sophisticated computer simulations of the sequence of events that occurred from the moment the aircraft struck the towers until they began to collapse, according to NIST.

More than 1,000 artifacts recovered: The Port Authority of New York & New Jersey preserved more than 1,000 artifacts recovered from the World Trade Center, according to the Port Authority. They are stored at John F. Kennedy International Airport's Hangar 17, an 80,000-square-foot facility.

Requests for debris: Port Authority spokesman Steve Coleman in a Port Authority report, MSNBC.

# Chapter 4: The Pentagon

## INTRODUCTION

Description of the Pentagon environs on 9/11: *The 9/11 Commission Report*, page 1; *Popular Mechanics* interview with Bill Hopper, Communications Manager, Pentagon Renovation & Construction Program, April 20, 2006; *The Pentagon Building Performance Report*, commissioned by the American Society of Civil Engineers (ASCE) and released in January 2003.

## FLIGHT 77 DEBRIS

Complete quote from Mike Walter, eyewitness to the Flight 77 crashing into the Pentagon: CNN transcript, September 11, 2001; *Popular Mechanics* interview with Walter, April 26, 2006.

William Lagasse's eyewitness account of the Flight 77 crash: ABC's *Nightline*, September 11, 2002.

Record of passenger calls from hijacked Flight 77: *The 9/11 Commission Report*.

DNA results of Flight 77 passengers found in Pentagon wreckage: Armed Forces Institute of Pathology report, November 16, 2001.

Description of Flight 77's impact on the Pentagon: *Popular Mechanics* interview with Paul Mlakar, April 21, 2006.

Information on the size of the Pentagon's concrete columns: *The Pentagon Building Performance Report*, Section 2.1.

Information on Pentagon renovations and construction: *Popular Mechanics* interview with Bill Hopper, April 20, 2006.

FBI protocol for securing evidence at a crash site: *Popular Mechanics* interviews with Matthew McCormick, former chief, Survival Factors Division, National Transportation Safety Board, November 30, 2004 and April 25, 2006; *Popular Mechanics* interview with Todd Curtis, founder, AirSafe.com, December 1, 2004.

Eyewitness account of Flight 77 wreckage by Allyn E. Kilsheimer, CEO, KCE Structural Engineers, Washington D.C.: *Popular Mechanics* interviews, December 7, 2004, and April 25, 2006.

## BIG PLANE, SMALL HOLES

Note: *The Pentagon Building Performance Report* cites the approximate dimensions of the Ring E hole as 90 feet in diameter. *Popular Mechanics* incorrectly reported the diameter as 75 feet in its March 2005 issue ("9/11: Debunking the Myths").

Description of Purdue University's computer simulation of the Flight 77 impact: Computer Graphics and Visualization Lab, Department of Computer Science, Purdue University, September 2002; *Popular Mechanics* interview with Mete Sozen, Kettelhut Distinguished Professor of Civil Engineering at Purdue University, April 17, 2006.

Frank Probst's eyewitness account of the Flight 77 crash: *The Pentagon Building Performance Report* (Section 3.2).

Don Mason's confirmation of Probst's account: *The Pentagon Building Performance Report* (Section 3.2).

Penny Elgas's eyewitness account: September 11: Bearing Witness to History Collection, National Museum of American History, Smithsonian Institution, Washington D.C. Before becoming a permanent collection, "Bearing Witness" was a Smithsonian exhibit that attracted more than 1 million people during its run from September 11, 2002, to July 6, 2003. The collection can be toured at www.americanhistory.si.edu/september11/index.asp. When curators asked visitors to record their experiences on the morning of 9/11, more than 20,600 people wrote accounts that are preserved in a digital archive at www.911digitalarchive.org/smithsonian.

Location of the flight data record: *The Pentagon Building Performance Report* (Section 6.1).

### INTACT PENTAGON WINDOWS

Description of blast-resistant windows: Ken Hays, executive vice president, Masonry Arts, Inc., Bessemer, Alabama: *Popular Mechanics* interviews, December 1, 2004 and April 20, 2006; *Popular Mechanics* interviews with Kilsheimer, December 7, 2004 and April 25, 2006; "Blast-resistant windows at Pentagon credited with saving lives," *Laminated Glass News*, May 20, 2004.

Description of Pentagon modernization: "Pentagon Renovation PenRen— Making the Biggest Better," Tom Inglesby, *Masonry Arts* magazine, August 2002; "Retrofitting the Pentagon for Blast Resistance," Michael N. Biscotte, P.E., and Keith A. Almoney, *Structure* magazine, July 2001.

# Chapter 5: Flight 93

### INTRODUCTION

Description of the hijacked airplanes' departures: *The 9/11 Commission Report*; *Perfect Soldiers: The 9/11 Hijackers: Who They Were, Why They Did It*, Terry McDermott.

Airplane loudspeaker transmissions: *The 9/11 Commission Report*.

Federal Aviation Administration (FAA) and chain of command: interview and e-mail correspondence with Laura Brown, spokeswoman, FAA, May 16, 2006; interview with Major Darren G. Steele, spokesman, NORAD, May 17, 2006.

Flight 93 passengers' phone communications: *Among the Heroes: United Flight 93 and the Passengers and Crew Who Fought Back*, Jere Longman; *The 9/11 Commission Report*.

### F-16 PILOT

Gibney flight location and schedule: e-mail correspondence with Master Sergeant David E. Somdahl, public information officer, 119th Fighter Wing, North Dakota Air National Guard, June 1, 2006; interview with Edward Jacoby Jr., former director of the New York State Emergency Management Office, May 26, 2006.

Gibney award presentation: interview with Edward Jacoby Jr., June 6, 2006.

Grand-Pre's allegations: interview with David E. Somdahl, May 26, 2006.

9/11 chain of command: *The 9/11 Commission Report*.

Domestic Events Network: interview with Laura Brown, spokeswoman, FAA, May 16, 2006.

### THE WHITE JET

VF Corporation airplane: interview with Yates Gladwell, airplane copilot, December 14, 2004; interview with David Newell, director of aviation and travel, VF Corporation, May 26, 2006.

Confirmation of no U.S. Customs aircraft in the vicinity of Flight 93: e-mail correspondence with Michael Friel, director, Border Security Media Division, U.S. Customs and Border Protection, Department of Homeland Security, June 2, 2002. On September 11, Friel notes, U.S. Customs had no aircraft anywhere near the route of Flight 93, no aircraft in the fleet that were armed, and none that could have matched the speed of an airliner.

### CELL-PHONE CALLS

Flight 93 phone calls: *Among the Heroes*; *The 9/11 Commission Report*.

Altitude phone technology: interview with Rick Kemper, director of wireless technology, CTIA—The Wireless Association (CTIA), May 23, 2006; interview with David Hoover, director of policy, CTIA, May 23 and 24, 2006; interview with Jeffery Nelson, spokesman, Verizon, May 22, 2006; interview with Debra Lewis, spokeswoman, Verizon, May 22, 2006.

Maximum altitude for cell-phone calls: interviews with Paul Guckian, vice president of engineering, Qualcomm, and Jeremy James, corporate communication spokesman, Qualcomm, May 23, 2006.

FAA cell-phone regulations: interview with Laura Brown and Alison Duquette, spokeswomen, FAA, May 16, 2006; interview with Tim Wagner, spokesman, American Airlines, May 22, 2006.

Description of cell-phone functioning: interview and e-mail correspondence with Rick Kemper, CTIA, May 23, 2006; interviews with Paul Guckian, Qualcomm, May 23, 2006.

Tom Burnett phone call: *Among the Heroes*. Burnett's wife Deena also includes transcripts of her conversations with her husband on 9/11 at www.tomburnettfoundation.org.

Flight 93 passengers calling loved ones: *Among the Heroes*; *The 9/11 Commission Report*.

CeeCee Lyles's call to her husband: *Among the Heroes*.

## THE WRECKAGE

Engine fan information: interview with Bill Crowley, special agent, FBI, May 29, 2006; interview with Paul Breslin, spokesman, FBI, May 26, 29, and 30, 2006; interview with Susan McKee, spokeswoman, FBI, May 26 and 29, 2006; interview with Matthew McCormick, former chief of Survival Factors Group, National Transportation Safety Board (NTSB), May 26, 2006; interview with Wallace Miller, coroner, Somerset County (Pennsylvania) Coroner's Office, May 31, 2006.

Rick King comments: *ABC News* clip, September 11, 2001.

Crash investigation: interviews with Greg Feith, crash investigator and former senior investigator, NTSB, May 23 and 26, 2006.

Flight 93 position at impact crash: *The 9/11 Commission Report*.

Flight 77 landing gear: interview with Paul Mlakar, senior research scientist, U.S. Army Corps of Engineers, April 14, 2006.

Crash site debris description: interview with Todd Curtis, director, www.airsafe.com, December 1, 2004.

## INDIAN LAKE

Location of human remains: interview with Jeff Reinbold, Flight 93 Memorial, May 30, 2006.

Site evidence: interview with Matt McCormick, NTSB, May 26, 2006.

Records of weather conditions on September 11: National Oceanic and Atmospheric Administration.

# Recommended 9/11 Web Sites

A wide range of online resources provide additional information on these and other 9/11 conspiracy claims:

The Middle East Media Research Institute addresses allegations of Israeli or Jewish involvement in 9/11 (which are particularly widespread in the Arab media) at www.memri.org.

The Political Research Association, a group dedicated to studying far-right political movements, offers a broad overview of 9/11 conspiracy theories at www.publiceye.org/conspire/conspiracism-911.html.

The National September 11 Memorial & Museum offers an interactive timeline of the day at timeline.national911memorial.org.

A variety of independent Web sites have emerged to present fact-based challenges to 9/11 conspiracy theories. These sites vary in quality, but show an admirable determination to counter misconceptions with verifiable data. Two of the best are:

www.geocities.com/debunking911/index.htm
www.911myths.com

The popularity of the documentary *Loose Change* has spurred several independent Web sites to tackle the film's many incorrect claims and illogical leaps. Here is one:

www.ccdominoes.com/lc/LooseChangeGuide.html

David Corn, the Washington editor for *The Nation*, has written extensively about 9/11 conspiracy theories. Here, he provides background on several leading theorists:

www.thenation.com/blogs/capitalgames?bid=3&pid=66

# INDEX

# ABOUT THE EDITORS

**DAVID DUNBAR** is the executive editor of *Popular Mechanics* and led the editorial team that produced the magazine's exposé of 9/11 conspiracy theories. He has also supervised the magazine's coverage of the war in Iraq and Hurricane Katrina, as well as aviation, military technology, and other topics.

**BRAD REAGAN** is a contributing editor to *Popular Mechanics*, reporting on counterterrorism, digital forensics, and law enforcement. He was previously a staff writer for *The Wall Street Journal*.